Pennsylvania
Off the Beaten Path®

Help Us Keep This Guide Up-to-Date

Every effort has been made by the author and editors to make this guide as accurate and useful as possible. However, many things can change after a guide is published—establishments close, phone numbers change, and facilities come under new management, etc.

We would love to hear from you concerning your experiences with this guide and how you think it could be improved and kept up-to-date. While we may not be able to respond to all comments and suggestions, we'll take them to heart, and we'll also make certain to share them with the author. Please send your comments and suggestions to the following address:

The Globe Pequot Press
Reader Response/Editorial Department
P.O. Box 480
Guilford, CT 06437

Or you may e-mail us at:
editorial@globe-pequot.com

Thanks for your input, and happy travels!

Pennsylvania

FIFTH EDITION

Off the Beaten Path®

by Susan Perloff

The Globe Pequot Press

Guilford, Connecticut

Pennsylvania Wineries listing reprinted in part from *Pennsylvania Wines and Wineries,* courtesy of the Pennsylvania Wine Association. Streets paved in red brick listing reprinted from *Philadelphia Almanac and Citizens' Manual,* courtesy of The Library Company of Philadelphia.

Cover and text design by Laura Augustine
Cover photo by Index Stock Imagery
Maps created by Equator Graphics © The Globe Pequot Press
Text illustrations by Carol Drong

Library of Congress Cataloging-in-Publication Data is available.

Perloff, Susan.
    Pennsylvania : off the beaten path / by Susan Perloff.—5th ed.
      p. cm. — (Off the beaten path series)
    Rev. ed. of: Pennsylvania / Sara Pitzer. 4th ed. c 1997.
    Includes index.
    ISBN 0-7627-0462-4
      1. Pennsylvania—Guidebooks. I. Pitzer, Sara. Pennsylvania. II. Title. III. Series.
F147.3 .P57 1999
917.4804'43—dc21

                    99-048818

Manufactured in the United States of America
Fifth Edition/Second Printing

*To my lovely husband, Ed,
and our sons, Joel, David, and Dan,
who keep me off the beaten path,
laughing all the way.*

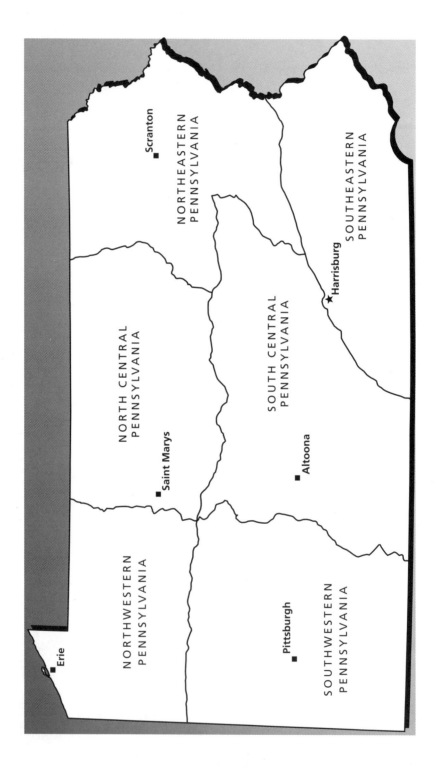

Contents

Acknowledgments

Thanks to Ed Blumstein and Jackie Purvis for reading every word. That's way above and beyond.

Thanks to the people who helped with research and ideas: Nancy Groff, Vicki and Don Kramer, Peg Laney, and Janet Burd. For help and support, thanks to Harry Cerino and Ken Finkel of the William Penn Foundation; Carrie Rickey, movie critic, *Philadelphia Inquirer;* Gene Blaum of the Pennsylvania Department of Transportation; Olga Herbert, executive director of the Lincoln Highway Heritage Corridor; Joan Montgomery and Gina Bertucci of Camelback Ski Area; and Rick Dunlap of Bozell Kamstra, Pittsburgh. To the scores of helpful, friendly folks at various tourist bureaus and visitors centers: *merci beaucoup.* You performed your job with a smile, making mine more pleasant.

For six years, Frank Rossi was my muse, inspiration, and chief editorial critic. He parsed my sentences, tightened my prose, and encouraged me to find my own voice in writing. Frank Rossi was raised in Scranton, Pennsylvania, lived on my block in Philadelphia, and built a vacation cabin in Hop Bottom in the Endless Mountains. He was a columnist for the *Philadelphia Inquirer.* Frank should have lived long enough to see my name on the cover of a book—or his own. Thanks, Frank, for being my friend. I miss you.

To the tree—I hope it was a Pennsylvania hardwood—that gave its life for research, producing brochures, newsletters, and maps that I received from every major and minor tourist attraction in the state. The pile of paper eventually rose more than a yard above my desk.

Introduction

Many years ago, before ZIP codes, before diet colas, before even *Howdy Doody*, I was born in Pennsylvania. My parents and three of my grandparents were born in Pennsylvania. My husband and our three sons were born in Pennsylvania. After high school, I attended the University of Pennsylvania, as did my parents, my sister, my husband, *his* sister, one son—and twenty-four other people related to us through marriage or divorce. Unless I missed some. Inbred? *Moi?*

I lived in Pennsylvania when Sputnik shot into orbit, when President Kennedy was assassinated, and when the Flyers won the Stanley Cup. Through thick and thin, through snowstorm and hurricane, through political controversy and the moving of the Liberty Bell, I remain.

Many of my friends have lived in other, more exotic places, like, say, Iowa, but we get along. My friend Jackie, for instance, was born in Hershey, Pennsylvania, where her father worked on the assembly line in the chocolate factory. Jackie has lived in three other states and two other countries. What I know about the Keystone State, she knows about Paris, Pakistan, and the Philippines, up close and personal. She has friends in Chicago and Cairo, while everyone I know is local. Of course, that means every time we go out, we run into someone I know.

Like—Ed Rendell, mayor of Philadelphia from 1992 to 2000, who was my classmate at Penn. I've been at a dinner party with United States Senator Arlen Specter and done volunteer work with Lynn Yeakel, who opposed him in the 1992 senatorial race. Deans of law schools, chairs of medical departments, owners of expensive restaurants, and people who can lay seamless, wall-to-wall carpet have crossed my path or my husband's in class, in interviews, or in the park. And I love it. Jackie can get an invitation to Kazakhstan any time she wants. But when I go to an outlet shopping center in the Poconos, I'm likely to run into the head nurse from the hospital where I worked twenty-five years ago. So if anyone should write a guidebook about Pennsylvania, I probably qualify.

My friend Peg puts another spin on this guidebook thing. Born in Virginia, Peg has lived in Massachusetts, Maine, and now New Jersey (we met during her Jersey period). She says some states have statewide identities (Texas does, Virginia and Maine do) while other states— notably Massachusetts and New Jersey—do not. Nor does Pennsylvania, it seems. Until now, at least for me. Researching the farther reaches of my native state has given me new awareness, new appreciation, and an increased need for vacation days to take it all in.

During colonial times Pennsylvania was the middle colony of the original thirteen colonies. It held the colonies together as the keystone supports the arch above a window or door, so it's the Keystone State. Actually, technically, it's not a state at all. Officially Pennsylvania is a commonwealth. The word comes from Old English and means the "common weal" or well-being of the public. In Pennsylvania, all legal processes are carried out in the name of the Commonwealth, although the word does not appear on the State Seal.

How to Use this Book

Mountains rise, gorges form, and towns develop. But they don't do so according to a highway map. As you read this book, please take the time to enjoy the Keystone State. Drive quickly if you must; take the humble, unpretentious roads if you can. Talk to people, listen, laugh, and enjoy. Breathe the clean air, admire the fall foliage, climb the mountains. We who live here love it. Hope you do, too.

The book is divided into six geographic sections. Attractions and locations are scattered within each section because, again, we didn't place the museums to suit the highways.

Pennsylvania Facts

Brief History of Early Pennsylvania

King Charles II of England gave William Penn, a Quaker, a large tract of land in the New World as repayment of a debt the king owed to William's father. The tract of land that became known as Pennsylvania, or "Penn's Woods," was settled in 1643. William Penn encouraged the Quakers and other persecuted groups to settle in Pennsylvania, saying "No person shall be molested or prejudiced for his or her conscientious persuasion or practice." In Pennsylvania, he promised, they could practice their religious beliefs in a democratic way. Over time, Pennsylvania's freedom appealed not only to Quakers but also to Amish, Moravians, Slovaks, Poles, Jews, Catholics, Hungarians, Italians, Irish, Greeks, and many other religious and ethnic groups.

Penn established a legislature, making his mark as one of America's great visionaries. "He was the greatest law-giver the world has produced," said Thomas Jefferson. William Penn originally intended the capital of Pennsylvania to be located in Upland, now known as Chester.

In 1682 the capital moved upriver to Philadelphia. But as settlers in Pennsylvania began pushing westward, legislators decided that the capital should be in a more central location, so they moved the capital to Lancaster in 1799 and finally to Harrisburg in 1810.

You Take the High Road, and I'll Take Route 30

Pennsylvania has the nation's fourth-largest highway system—more than 44,000 miles of highways under state control. And the Keystone State has the eighth-highest count of highway miles—nearly 119,000 miles. Bottom line: It's *real* easy to get around. From four-lane highways with limited access to country roads that pass more cows than people, Pennsylvania has its share of concrete, macadam, and tarmac.

Among all this mileage, five highways deserve special attention:

1. The National Road (Route 40) was the first federally funded highway (1818 to 1835). It connected Washington, D.C., with points west, traversing Maryland, cutting across the southwest corner of Pennsylvania, visiting Ohio and Indiana, and ending in Illinois. The National Road opened up land west of the Alleghenies and allowed a budding nation to expand westward. Today the National Road Heritage Park (NRHP) celebrates the history and heritage of Route 40. You can see tollhouses in Petersburg and Searights and nearly fifty more structures that served as taverns and inns during the road's early years. For the small-town charm of yesteryear, visit the historical districts of Uniontown, Brownsville, Addison, and Claysville. Write to the NRHP at 3543 National Road, Farmington 15437. You can call (724) 329–1560 or speed through www.hhs.net/nrhp.

2. The Lincoln Highway (Route 30) was the first coast-to-coast highway. When it was established in 1913, it was merely a line on a map, stretching from New York City to San Francisco by connecting existing roads. In 1925 the government began numbering highways. In 1928 the Lincoln Highway Association fabricated and installed (with the help of Boy Scouts) more than 3,000 concrete markers—one at almost every mile—all across the country. Bands of red, white, and blue (with a big *L*) were painted on telephone poles to designate the highway. Alas, road widenings, snow plows, and other natural disasters have destroyed all but about twenty markers. The Lincoln Highway Heritage Corridor (LHHC), a nonprofit organization, aims to encourage you to follow this ribbon of highway, where you'll discover nifty attractions that your grandparents might have seen. Within Pennsylvania, Route 30 covers 320 miles and thirteen counties. At its westernmost Pennsylvania point, it's 4 miles west of Hookstown; it travels east through the state and crosses the Benjamin Franklin Bridge from Philadelphia to Camden, New Jersey. Reach LHHC at Box 386, Greensburg 15601. You can call (724) 837–9750, fax (724) 837–9751, or visit www.lhhc.org.

3. U.S. Route 6. It ain't Route 66, but you can get your kicks on this highway, which cuts an impressive swath from Port Jervis on the east, where New York and New Jersey meet the Keystone State. It keeps going east through New Jersey, New York, and Connecticut, terminating in New Bedford, Rhode Island. On the west, Route 6 leaves Pennsylvania at Pennline. It visits Cleveland, Ohio, and Minturn, Colorado, and never slows down until it reaches Bishop, California (though at some spots, it's subsumed into the behemoth interstate highway).

4. U.S. Route 1. Don't forget this classic roadway, which spends about 75 miles in Southeastern Pennsylvania, much of it an endless, repetitive strip mall. But Route 1 goes on and on and on. It runs from Madawaska, way up at the tippy-top of Northern Maine, down to Key West, Florida, home of Jimmy Buffet and romantic sunsets. Depending whether you're cold-blooded or warm-blooded you can say it begins or ends in the north or south. Whatever. It's a highly traveled road—often supplanted, but rarely improved, by I–95.

5. The Pennsylvania Turnpike. How come Paul Simon sang about the New Jersey Turnpike and not the Pennsylvania Turnpike, the nation's first four-lane, limited-access superhighway? Construction was sparked by the need to put unemployed people to work during the Great Depression. The turnpike followed a long-abandoned right-of-way left over from a nineteenth century railroad war and eventually served as the prototype for the interstate highway system. The original Pennsylvania Turnpike ran from Irwin to Carlisle and had no speed limit. In the 1950s families traveled on the turnpike just to have dinner at one of the service plazas. The Pennsylvania Turnpike developed the Sonic Nap Alert Pattern (SNAP), which is the placement of rumble strips along the edge of the right lane to alert drivers who are falling asleep. Innovation continues: In 1999 the turnpike began accepting advertising on its toll receipts.

Delightful Driving Tours Recommended by the Pennsylvania Office of Travel and Tourism

Northern Zone

Route 6 from Smethport through Coudersport to Galeton

Route 44 from Coneville through Cherry Springs State Park to Oleona

Route 15 from Liberty through Mansfield to Tioga

Route 6 from Towanda to Factoryville

I–81 from Hallstead to East Benton

Central Zone

Route 26 from State College to Huntingdon

Route 62 from Tideoute (rhymes with *pretty suit*) to Oil City

Route 322 from Clearfild to Potters Mills

Route 42 from Eagles Mere through Bloomsburg to Mount Carmel

Route 422 from Kittanning through Indiana to Ebensburg

Route 30 from Ligonier to Schellsburg

Southern Zone

Route 30 from Gettysburg to Bedford

Route 32 along the Delaware River from Easton to Yardley

Route 233 from Mont Alto through Pine Grove Furnace to Landisburg

Route 10 from Reading through Honey Brook to Cochanville

Route 445 from Fort Hunter through Pine Grove to Route 895 to Bowmanstown

The Mason Dixon Line

The English astronomers Charles Mason and Jeremiah Dixon surveyed parts of the colonies in the 1760s and drew a straight line—the stripe that became the Mason Dixon Line. Pennsylvania touches the north side of the line; Delaware, Maryland, and West Virginia touch the south. During the Civil War, the North, the Union, were the "free states," and the South, the Confederacy, were the "slave states."

Pennsylvania's Welcome Centers

The Pennsylvania Department of Transportation (PennDot) and the Pennsylvania Turnpike Commission operate Welcome Centers at highway entrances to the Keystone State. Knowledgeable and friendly hosts at the centers can offer directional assistance; provide detailed information about Pennsylvania's culture, history, scenic attractions, and activities; give you the weather forecast; report on road conditions; and arrange overnight accommodations. The centers have vending machines, picnic tables, rest rooms, and pet areas. The Welcome Centers operate from 8:30 A.M. to 5:00 P.M., seven days a week, including most holidays.

Claysville, I–70 eastbound, 5 miles west of West Virginia border.

Easton, I–78 westbound, 1 mile west of New Jersey border.

Edinboro, I–79 southbound, 1 mile south of Edinboro exit.

Kirby, I–79 northbound, 5 miles north of West Virginia border.

Lenox, I–81 southbound, 4 miles south of exit 64.

Linwood, I–95 northbound, $1/2$ mile north of Delaware border.

Matamoras, I–84 at Exit 11.

Neshaminy Pennsylvania Turnpike, mile marker 51 westbound, 7 miles west of New Jersey border.

Shrewsbury, I–83 northbound, $1/2$ mile north of Maryland border.

Sideling Hill Pennsylvania Turnpike, mile marker 172, 10 miles east of Breezewood exit.

State Line, I–81 northbound, $1^1/2$ miles north of Maryland border.

Warfordsburg, I–70 westbound, $1/2$ mile east of Maryland border.

West Middlesex, I–80 eastbound, $1/2$ mile east of Ohio border.

Zelienople Pennsylvania Turnpike, mile marker 21 eastbound, 21 miles east of Ohio border.

Kid's Corner

Caution: This information may be offensive to anyone over age twelve. Then again, it may not. If you are in or near Pennsylvania any weekday evening at 7:00, tune in to *Kid's Corner*, a daily call-in program for children. The amiable, patient, and endlessly inventive Kathy O'Connell encourages kids to laugh, ask silly questions, sing songs about alien babies, and pick up stray facts. One night Kathy plays "My Hair Had a Party Last Night," by her favorite musical group, Trout Fishing in America. Another evening she invites a pediatrician to discuss colds, then insists on differentiating between snot and boogers. The show is never boring. More than 40,000 kids call each month, making *Kid's Corner* the most popular children's program on public radio. Find it on WXPN–FM, 88.5, Philadelphia; WXPH–FM, 88.1, Harrisburg; and WKHS–FM, 90.5, Whorton, Maryland.

You've Got a Friend Who Eats in Pennsylvania: Eleven Keystone Food Firsts

1861   Julius Sturgis Pretzel Company, Lititz, becomes America's first commercial baker.

1894   Cracker Jacks are first manufactured in Philadelphia.

1900   Frank Fleer coats chewing gum in sugar. *Voilà*: Chicklets.

1902   Fast food is born at the Horn & Hardart Automat, 818 Chestnut Street, Philadelphia.

1904   The banana split makes its appearance in Latrobe.

1918   Frank Fleer does it again: Dubble Bubble.

1920   Emil's, 1800 South Broad Street, Philadelphia, makes sandwiches for Hog Island workers and calls them hoagies.

1929   Sam Isaly of Pittsburgh creates the Klondike, the first ice cream bar, selling it for a nickel.

1936   Frank Ludens of Reading manufactures the Fifth Avenue Candy Bar.

1937   Good 'n' Plenty Candy is manufactured in Philadelphia.

1968   Jim Delligatti, a McDonald's franchise owner, invents the Big Mac in Uniontown.

Fun Food Fact: How sweet it is. Chocolate factories in Pennsylvania include Blommer, in East Greenville; Godiva, in Reading; Goldenberg, in Philadelphia; Hershey, in Hershey; Mars, in Elizabethtown; R.M. Palmer, in West Reading; and Wilbur, in Lititz. Does that make it the Keystone Sweet?

Pennsylvania's Official Designations

Animal: Whitetail Deer

Beverage: Milk

Bird: Ruffed Grouse

Dog: Great Dane

Fish: Brook Trout

Flower: Mountain Laurel

Fossil: Phacops Rana

Insect: Firefly

Motto: Virtue, Liberty, and Independence

Ship: United States Brig *Niagara*

Tree: Hemlock

Geography

Area: 45,888 square miles

Campsites: 7,000

Capital: Harrisburg, in Dauphin County

Counties: 67

Counties with no traffic lights: Forest and Perry

Geographic center: Centre County, 2 $^1/_2$ miles southwest of Bellefonte

Highest point: Mt. Davis, 3,213 feet

Lakes: 50 natural lakes (over 20 acres wide) and 2,500 artificial lakes

Largest county: Lycoming, which is larger than Rhode Island

Lowest point: Delaware River

Miles of Appalachian Trail: 230 (The midpoint of 2,144-mile Appalachian Trail, where it's traditional to eat a half gallon of ice cream, is in Pine Grove Furnace State Park, Cumberland County.)

Rivers with the hardest-to-pronounce names: Schuylkill (say *school kill*) and Youghiogheny (rhymes with *sock a say knee*) rivers

Rivers and streams: 45,000 miles, more flowing water than any other continental state

Species of fish: 159

Species of trees: 127

State forest districts: 20; acreage: 2,200,000

State game lands: 294; acreage: 1,379,002

State parks: 116; acreage: 282,500; miles of trails: 5,000

Size: 310 miles (east to west), 180 miles (north to south)

Pennsylvania Government

U.S. Representatives: 21

State Representatives: 203

State Senators: 50

Elected officials: 12,294

Municipalities: 2,569 (more than any other state)

Sales tax on clothing: Zero

Pennsylvania Firsts

First all motion–picture theater

First druggist

First educational public television station

First hospital—Pennsylvania Hospital

First locomotive for railroad use

First national capital—Philadelphia

First newspaper

First paper mill

First television broadcast

First zoo—Zoological Society of Philadelphia

Agriculture (the state's largest industry)

Farms: 55,000

Farmland: 9,000,000 acres

Rural population: 3,700,000

Leading farm products: dairy products, mushrooms, apples, tobacco, grapes, peaches, cut flowers

Pig farmers: 4,500

Pigs: 1,000,000

Counties that do not raise pigs: only Philadelphia, Delaware, and Pike counties; the other sixty-four counties raise pigs

Mascots of Major Sports Teams

- **Philadelphia Phillies**—Phanatic
- **Philadelphia 76'ers**—Hot Shot
- **Philadelphia Phantoms**—Phantom
- **Pittsburgh Pirates**—Pirate
- **Philadelphia Eagles**—Eagle

Famous Natives and Residents

Louisa May Alcott, *novelist*

Marian Anderson, *contralto*

Samuel Barber, *composer*

John Barrymore, *actor*

Donald Barthelme, *author*

Stephen Vincent Benet, *poet and story writer*

Daniel Boone, *frontiersman*

Ed Bradley, *TV anchorman*

James Buchanan, *U.S. president*

Alexander Calder, *sculptor*

Rachel Carson, *biologist and author*

Mary Cassatt, *painter*

Henry Steele Commager, *historian*

Bill Cosby, *actor*

Jimmy and Tommy Dorsey, *band leaders*

W. C. Fields, *comedian*

Stephen Foster, *composer*

Robert Fulton, *inventor*

Grace, *Princess of Monaco*

Martha Graham, *choreographer*

Alexander Haig, *former secretary of state*

Marilyn Horne, *mezzo-soprano*

Lee Iacocca, *auto executive*

Reggie Jackson, *baseball player*

Gene Kelly, *dancer and actor*

S. S. Kresge, *merchant*

Mario Lanza, *actor and singer*

Margaret Mead, *anthropologist*

Andrew Mellon, *financier*

Tom Mix, *actor*

Arnold Palmer, *golfer*

Robert E. Peary, *explorer*

Man Ray, *painter*

Betsy Ross, *flagmaker*

B. F. Skinner, *psychologist*

John Sloan, *painter*

Gertrude Stein, *author*

James Stewart, *actor*

John Updike, *novelist*

Fred Waring, *band leader*

Ethel Waters, *singer and actress*

Anthony Wayne, *military officer*

August Wilson, *poet, writer, and playwright*

Wallis Warfield, *Duchess of Windsor*

Andrew Wyeth, *painter*

When Autumn Leaves Start to Fall

A magnificent time to be in Pennsylvania is during the autumn, when 127 varieties of trees change from summer green into 127 spectacularly brilliant fall colors. Choose this time to hike a nature trail—breathing the clean, crisp air, experiencing the beauty of the red maples, comparing falling leaves. If two feet are not the way you want to experience autumn in Pennsylvania, how about two wheels?

Annual Temperature Averages (Fahrenheit): Maximum/Minimum

	Lehigh County	Erie County	Dauphin County	Philadelphia
January	32/18	27/16	34/22	35/20
April	66/43	61/42	67/46	67/56
July	83/63	78/62	85/67	85/66
October	65/44	63/46	65/49	69/50
	Allegheny County	Luzerne County	Lycoming County	Wayne County
January	29/16	29/14	30/16	30/15
April	67/43	62/41	66/41	65/40
July	80/60	80/60	82/60	80/60
October	65/45	62/43	63/48	62/47

The prices and rates listed in this guidebook were confirmed at press time. We recommend, however, that you call establishments before traveling to obtain current information.

Southeastern Pennsylvania: Philadelphia and Its Countryside

Philadelphia

How do you introduce a major metropolis to strangers without driving them around in your car? Do you start with the history? The planned geography? The parks and zoo? Or your favorite restaurants in a city overflowing with A-1 eateries in all price ranges?

Philadelphia is the fifth-largest city in the country and the fourth-largest metro area. The region comprises five counties in Pennsylvania (Bucks, Chester, Delaware, Montgomery, and Philadelphia) plus two in New Jersey (Camden and Gloucester). In the sixties Walter Annenberg, who then owned the *Philadelphia Inquirer* and *Daily News*, coined the phrase "Delaware Valley," essentially for marketing purposes. The term stuck for decades but has recently fallen out of favor. Now it's safe, once again, to refer to the Philadelphia region or the Philadelphia metropolitan area.

Philadelphia (most locals will thank you not to call it "Philly") was not always a bustling urban center of twelve million people. When William Penn received a gift of a lot of forestland in the New World—hence, Penn's Woods, or Pennsylvania—he became a seventeenth-century land speculator.

> ### Trivia
>
> *"Okay, I confess. I fell in love while I was making a movie. It happened in Philadelphia. When you're this much in love there's no place to go but back."*
>
> —Oprah Winfrey

> ### Trivia
>
> *"I love warm places, like Philadelphia. There's nothing warmer than the hearts of the people who live here. My friends, come visit the warmest place on earth."*
>
> —Bill Cosby

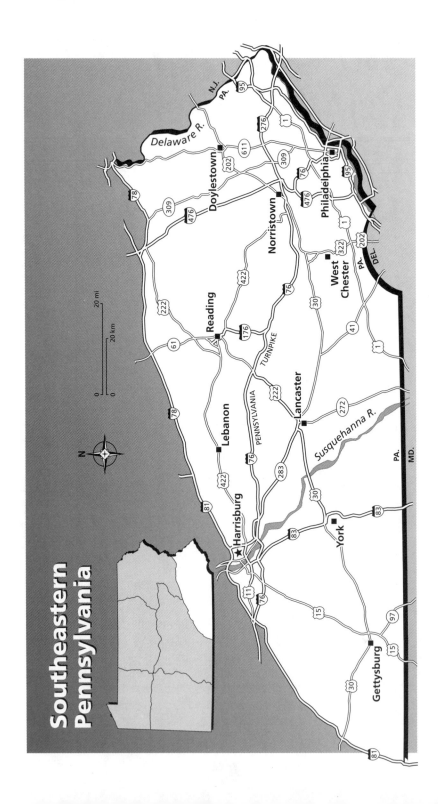

Southeastern Pennsylvania

AUTHOR'S TOP TEN FAVORITES IN SOUTH-EASTERN PENNSYLVANIA

Distelfinks

Philadelphia City Hall

The murals in Philadelphia

Crayola Factory

Mincemeat pie from Groff's Meats

Philadelphia Museum of Art Craft Show

Hawk Mountain

Jill's Vorspeise

Walking across the Benjamin Franklin Bridge to New Jersey

Statue of Ben Franklin on Penn's campus

William Penn perceived his burgh to be a "greene countrie towne." In his 2-miles-wide-by-1-mile-north/south plan, Penn arranged for five squares to remain forever green. Four of those—Logan in the northwest, Rittenhouse in the southwest, Washington in the southeast, and Franklin in the northeast—remain gardeny (and all but Franklin make delightful strolls, meeting places, or picnic sites). In the central square, cleverly called Center Square, the city built its *City Hall* in 1871. The building sits at the crossroads of the city and holds the mayor's office, city council, and courtrooms. The place is hardly off the beaten path, but few people think of it as a tourist destination, which it assuredly is. Treat yourself to a tour.

City Hall

ity Hall, the biggest slice of gingerbread you'll ever see, always knew what it wanted to be when it grew up: the tallest, most impressive building in Philadelphia, dominating the skyline by its height and the sidewalks by its magnitude, and the tallest building in the world. Although the structure fulfilled its local expectations for four-score years, in 1987 an upstart developer got permission to build higher. Now seven prosaic office towers dwarf the seat of municipal government. As for being the tallest structure in the world, though—no success. The blueprints called for Earth's biggest building, but by the end of the thirty-year construction, the Eiffel Tower and the Washington Monument had sprouted. It was the tallest *occupied* structure in the United States until 1909. Today City Hall is the world's highest masonry-bearing structure, which means it's the tallest building without steel supports. Tallest or not, "the marble elephant," now a National Historic Landmark, still inspires onlookers. Not long ago it won second place in a *Philadelphia Inquirer* poll of readers' favorite buildings.

City Hall is a bold example of what architectural historians call high Victorian picturesque eclecticism, designed in the then-popular French Second Empire style, similar to the Old Executive Office Building next door to the White House. The

Trivia

Park your car and ride the **Phlash,** *a small van that makes thirty-three touristic stops in Center City. It operates every ten or fifteen minutes from 10:00 A.M. to 6:00 P.M. and costs $1.50 one way or $3.00 for an all-day pass. Call (215) 474–5274 for more details.*

most dominant part of City Hall is the Tower, soaring 548 feet above the ground. On top perches William Penn, sometimes called the tallest man in Philadelphia. Penn's 37-foot bronze likeness weighs more than twenty-six tons. He faces northeast, where the founder of Philadelphia and Pennsylvania made a legendary treaty with the Lenni Lenape Indians in 1682. You can ride to the visitors' platform thirty stories up, but plan to be patient—the tower elevator holds only seven people. Between 9:30 A.M. and 4:00 P.M., business days, take the elevator in the northeast corner to the seventh floor. Follow the red linoleum line on the floor and ride up an escalator. If the line's too long, get a ticket for a later lift. As you ride the glass-walled elevator up to the observation deck, check your

View from the Top

*A*s you emerge from the elevator at the top of the tower, you are facing south. If the guide can't help you determine what's what, there's probably a Philadelphian or two in the group who can. If you spend your allotted twelve minutes circling counterclockwise, here are some highlights of the view:

• *South Broad Street, the lower half of the reputed longest straight street in the world (15 miles, broken midway by the building you're in).*

• *Seven miles south, the sports complex, where the Army-Navy football game takes place and the Live-Aid concert happened.*

• *The gray Walt Whitman Bridge across the Delaware River to New Jersey.*

• *PSFS, which used to stand for the Philadelphia Savings Fund Society, which was gulped up by another bank. Philadelphians insisted that the sign stay up on the award-winning Art Deco building, which is now being converted to a hotel.*

• *The blue Benjamin Franklin Bridge to Camden. You may walk across:*

$1^8/_{10}$ *miles each way, daylight hours. No charge.*

• *The Pennsylvania Convention Center, a tan roof over 3 city blocks.*

• *The Masonic Temple, worth a guided tour, free, Monday to Friday, at 10:00 and 11:00 A.M. and 1:00, 2:00, and 3:00 P.M.. It's at 1 North Broad Street; telephone (215) 988–1917. The 1873 building includes Corinthian, Italian Renaissance, and Egyptian rooms.*

• *North on Broad, the other half of the longest straight street; $^1/_2$-mile up on the left is the white tower of the* Philadelphia Inquirer *and* Daily News.

• *The Benjamin Franklin Parkway, culminating in the Philadelphia Museum of Art, which sits above the steps Rocky climbed in his first movie.*

• *The seven loftier-than-thou office towers.*

• *The Schuylkill River.*

The Philadelphia Negro

*I*n 1899 W. E. B. DuBois published The Philadelphia Negro, *a meticulously researched, groundbreaking study of African-American life. The book, now a recognized classic in its field, was ignored by the people who sponsored it. The twenty-seven-year-old, spats-wearing, cane-carrying Victorian-looking gentleman researched the 40,000 African-Americans who lived amid more than a million whites in Philadelphia, then the second largest city in the nation.*

Seiko against the tower clock, which began ticking January 1, 1899. The north, south, east, and west clock faces are 23 feet across; each minute hand is 15 feet long, and each hour hand is 12$^{1}/_{2}$ feet long.

City Hall has seven complete floors, two partial floors, and a basement, though the oversized windows and columns make it look like a three-story structure. The first interior level is tall enough for four pro basketball players to stand on one another's shoulders and not be able to reach the ceiling tiles. City Hall has more than 700 rooms, all with windows facing a street or an interior courtyard. If you don't do windows, imagine not doing 1,380 of them. Inside and out, City Hall boasts the richest sculptural decoration of any American building. The sculptor of Penn and the other 250 pieces was Alexander Milne Calder, father of the designer of the Swann Fountain at Philadelphia's Logan Circle and grandfather of the man credited with inventing mobiles.

The Foundation for Architecture runs one-and-one-half-hour tours, weekdays at 12:30 P.M. Enter the east portal and go to Room 121, where tours begin and where a gift shop offers souvenirs. The Foundation periodically leads exterior tours, also lasting one-and-one-half hours, which meet at the Visitors Center, Sixteenth Street and Kennedy Boulevard. For information on Foundation tours, call (215) 569–3187. For a taped recording, call (215) 569–8687, or write to the Foundation at 1737 Chestnut Street, Philadelphia 19103. If you're lucky, the guide on duty will be Greta Greenberger, who has done so much to preserve and promote this masterpiece that some people call her the Queen of City Hall. Try it. She'll like it. Actually, the Foundation runs dozens of other popular architectural tours, too, so you can check to see if the tour on, say, architectural terra-cotta, is available when you are.

The *Philadelphia Museum of Art* is a must-see, but timing is optional. For an off-the-beaten-time opportunity, try Wednesday evenings, when, in addition to seeing the paintings, you can participate in a special event

"People ask me why a girl from Massachusetts designed a scarf for Philadelphia. I tell them I stole the idea. I stole the hot pink from a sunset over the Philadelphia Museum of Art. I stole the soft blue from the shutters on an old house in Society Hill. I was overwhelmed by the beauty of the city. It was a crime of passion."

—Nicole Miller

that includes a film, dance instruction, a gallery talk, and storytelling—all for the normal museum entrance fee of $8.00 per adult. Light supper costs extra. Call (215) 763–8100 to find out what's on tap on the Wednesday of your choice.

In the art department, don't miss the **Clothespin** (as in "meet me at the Clothespin"), an oversized sculpture by artist Claes Oldenburg. It's at the corner of Fifteenth and Market Streets. Oldenburg's colossal **Button** is on the campus of the University of Pennsylvania, nearest the intersection of Thirty-fourth and Walnut Streets. And a few blocks west, at the pedestrian-only intersection of Locust Walk and Thirty-seventh Street, have a seat on the bronze bench next to the bronze statue of Benjamin Franklin, founder of the University. Ben's reading his *Pennsylvania Gazette*, leaning on his cane and waiting for you to relax. He's knows he's a photo op beyond compare.

For lunch, on City Hall day or any day, you can't beat the **Reading Terminal Market**. Founded in 1892 at the terminus of the Reading Railroad, this is a traditional stall market with eighty-five merchants selling usual and unique kinds of fish, meat, produce, pastries, flowers, and more. That's far fewer than the 800 stalls that lined the place on opening day, but it's big enough to find precisely the spice or the sourdough roll you want. The market is particularly known for its Pennsylvania Dutch vendors, who bring cheese and carrots from the surrounding countryside each day. It's open daily except Sunday from 8:00 A.M. to 6:00 P.M. Many stands sell delicious lunches at reasonable prices. One great choice is **Jill's Vorspeise** (215–925–5415) for soups, sandwiches, and roll-ups.

Please go out of your way to walk or drive through the **Friendship Gate** at Tenth and Arch Streets. It's the entrance to Chinatown, and it's just around the corner from the Reading Terminal Market.

An undiscovered urban treasure is the **Atwater Kent Museum**, whose collection details the people, places, and products of Philadelphia's 300-year history. There's a gift shop, too. Open daily except Tuesday, 10:00 A.M. to 4:00 P.M. Closed New Year's, Day, Martin Luther King Day, Thanksgiving, and Christmas; admission $3.00 for adults (15 South Seventh Street, just around the corner from Independence Hall; (215) 922– 3031). If you can't find it—check your map again. Don't bother to ask Philadelphians, even those walking by the front door. They've never heard of the Atwater Kent.

Go to jail. Go directly to jail. Do not pass *Go*, and do not miss a tour of the **Eastern State Penitentiary**, at Twenty-second Street and Fairmount Avenue. You can stay for a short time, unlike Al Capone and Willie Sutton (who robbed banks because, he said, that's where the money was). This was the world's first *penitentiary*, a place where criminals could be *penitent*. Constructed in the 1820s to rehabilitate criminals through solitary confinement, the castle-like prison that was once the most expensive building and most famous prison in the world, is now a crumbling, empty block of sky-lit cells and guard towers. Times of tours, which cost $7.00 per adult, vary seasonally. Call (215) 236–3300.

At Forty-third Street and Baltimore Avenue, in the pocket-sized Clark Park, is a **statue of Charles Dickens**, the only known sculpture in the world of the English author of *David Copperfield* and *Great Expectations*.

Edgar "Painless" Parker, a dentist with a perverse sense of humor, collected all the teeth he pulled at his chain of West Coast offices in the first

Films Shot in Whole or in Part in Philadelphia

Age of Innocence	1992	*Philadelphia*	1993
A Kiss before Dying	1991	*Philadelphia Story*	1940
Atlantic City	1980	*Rocky*	1976
Beyond the Walls	1950	*Taps*	1981
Birdy	1984	*Tattoo*	1980
Blow Out	1981	*The Blob*	1958
Burglar	1956	*The Soldier*	1982
Clean and Sober	1988	*The Trouble with Angels*	1966
David and Lisa	1963	*Trading Places*	1983
Dead Poets' Society	1989	*12 Monkeys*	1995
Dead Reckoning	1947	*Two Bits*	1993
"In" Crowd	1988	*Two Plus One*	1993
Kitty Foyle	1940	*Up Close and Personal*	1996
Lost in America	1984	*Witness*	1985
My Little Girl	1985	*Worth Winning*	1988
Nasty Habits	1977	*Young Philadelphians*	1959

half of the nineteenth century. You can see a bucket of these teeth at Temple University's **Dental Museum**, Broad Street and Allegheny Avenue. The museum occupies the dental school's three lobbies, and admission is free, weekdays 8:30 A.M. to 4:30 P.M. An authentic Victorian dental office makes a great, painless history lesson for kids. For more information call (215) 707–2816.

Fairmount Park

hiladelphia boasts **Fairmount Park,** the biggest planned urban park system in the world, with more than 8,700 acres of parkland, including natural and historical features, cultural attractions, recreation areas, and waterways. Every Philadelphian lives within a few

Philadelphia: The Mesopotamia of the Arts

arrie Rickey, syndicated movie critic for the Philadelphia Inquirer, *calls Philadelphia the Mesopotamia of the Arts. In a fifteen-minute conversation, she reels off the names of some of the city's contributions to the performing arts:*

- *Mario Lanza, singer and movie actor*

- *Nicholas Brothers, Fayard and Harold, African-American dancers*

- *Jeanette McDonald, actress*

- *Katharine Hepburn, who attended Bryn Mawr College*

- *Candice Bergen, who attended the University of Pennsylvania (and took two writing classes with the author)*

- *Bill Cosby, who needs no introduction*

- *Will Smith, actor*

- *W.C. Fields*

- *Elaine May, born here*

- *Grace Kelly, actress, later Princess of Monaco*

- *Sydney Lumet, movie director*

- *Brian dePalma, movie director*

- *Richard Brooks, directed In Cold Blood and Blackboard Jungle*

- *Garrett Brown, invented the Steadicam, "the most important addition to film technology since the introduction of sound," says Carrie Rickey*

- *Sylvester Stallone, attended high school here.*

- *Plus, in other categories.*

- *Binyamin Netanyahu, former prime minister of Israel, and his brother, Jonathan, who died in 1976 leading the successful rescue mission in Entebbe; attended high school here*

- *Willi Smith, clothing designer*

American Bandstand

American Bandstand, the TV show you watched after school in the late fifties if you were between the ages of ten and twenty, was a Philadelphia phenom. The rock 'n' roll dance party, which went national in 1957, starred sock-hoppers and Dick Clark, the host with the most. The 1947 building (now demolished) at Forty-sixth and Market Streets in West Philadelphia, where Chubby Checker chugged and played, was one of the first facilities designed and constructed exclusively for TV productions.

minutes of a park, and it's a rare citizen who doesn't have a favorite tree, path, or picnic spot. Out-of-towners who come here to see the Liberty Bell and then trot off to New York or Washington are missing a jewel if they skip the park.

A few years ago my sister and I donated a bench in Fairmount Park to our father's memory. It's on the West River Drive, at Black Rock Road. It faces upstream, with a view of the Strawberry Mansion Bridge and the regatta course. The plaque says FOR HERB NAGLER, WHO WILL ALWAYS LIVE FOR US IN FAIRMOUNT PARK. LOVE, SUZE AND JANE. Please visit.

The perfect trip to Philadelphia includes a visit to **Valley Green**—if you can find it. It's the best—absolutely the best—part of the superb park system. It's in the Wissahickon Valley, Wissahickon being an anglicized blend of two words used by the Lenni Lenape Indians; one meant yellow stream, the other meant catfish creek. (Anglers still occasionally lure catfish.) At Valley Green so many toddlers feed the ducks so many days of the year that the mallards can safely rely on human handouts for their livelihood. A 5-mile-long, dirt-and-gravel path, called **Forbidden Drive**, passes through Valley Green. It's called Forbidden Drive because it has always been forbidden to automobiles, and limited to walkers, runners, and horses, and now bikers and bladers. Valley Green, a totally un-urban Eden in the upper northwest section of the city, is always open. Study your map. Take Germantown Avenue northwest to #7900, turn left on Springfield Avenue, and follow signs (and the topography downhill) to the valley. Or take Henry Avenue northwest to #7900, then right on Wise's Mill Road, following signs to the valley. If you're on foot, access Forbidden Drive anywhere and stop for coffee or crepes at the **Valley Green Inn**. On a recent spring-like autumn day, a party of twelve overtook the porch, delighting in the walnut waffles, the people parade, and the falling leaves. Call (215) 247–1730 for reservations.

Trivia

"What a backyard I had growing up. Boathouse Row, Independence Hall. Come play in my old backyard. You'll love it, and I know it'll love you."

—Kevin Bacon

Pennypack Environmental Center manages a one-hundred-plus-acre nature center that was dedicated as a bird sanctuary in 1958. Near the building are a bird blind, an herb garden, a composting area, and a campfire area. Organized programs include bird walks, botany hikes, and craft sessions. The Environmental Center is located in the Far Northeast section of Philadelphia on Verree Road, 1 mile north of Rhawn Street and 1½ miles south of Red Lion Road.

Just upstream from the Art Museum is the **Fairmount Waterworks**, a steam-powered pumping station built nearly two centuries ago to supply drinking water for the growing city. The Engine House, which sits under the largest building, was completed in 1812. The Old Mill House that sits under the beautiful Greek-style buildings was completed in 1822. The caretaker's house, which sits next to the mansion, and the Watering Committee Building, its twin at the end of the row, were completed the same year.

The surrounding countryside, with its rolling hills and view of the Schuylkill River, soon became a popular attraction for tourists and

Follow the Red Brick Roads

F or a trip back in time, visit these twenty streets still paved in red brick. (List courtesy of the Library Company of Philadelphia, reprinted from Philadelphia Almanac and Citizens' Manual.*)*

Abbotsford Avenue (100 block)

Bodine Street (South 900)

Burbridge Street (6300)

Carlisle Street (5100 to 5300)

Chang Street (North 900)

Estaugh Street (West 100)

Fulton Street (South 600)

Gates Street (100)

Hedge Street (5300)

Jessup Street (South 200)

Lofty Street (200)

Maiden Street (100)

Montgomery Avenue (2900)

Orianna Street (300)

Pechin Street (4500)

Perkiomen Street (800)

Rector Street (100)

Smick Street (4800)

Wyneva Street (West 100)

Zeralda Street (300)

residents alike. The city developed the area into a park and installed walkways and fountains. The Gazebo was built in 1835 at the end of the dam. Many artists came to capture the scenic view, creating paintings that made the Fairmount Waterworks and Lemon Hill world famous. The city later bought two stately park mansions, Lemon Hill and the Sedgley Estate,

The Hebrew word Shalom *means* hello, goodbye, *and* peace. *The Philadelphia word* Yo! *covers roughly the same territory, plus* How ya doin'? *and* What's up? *or the shorter version,* 'Sup?

and in 1855 officially created Fairmount Park. As new and more advanced pumping stations were built, the Fairmount Waterworks closed in 1909. Two years later, the city turned the Old Mill House into an aquarium, which entertained children for several decades. When Philadelphia built an aquarium in South Philadelphia in the 1960s, the buildings were closed and fell into disrepair.

Several ill-fated renovation attempts have come and gone, but now rehab seems to be happening. With renewed interest in historic restoration and funding from several public and private organizations, the sorry-looking Waterworks has a good chance of survival. Hopefully, future generations will enjoy the scenic walkways and engineering marvels of this historic site, which has been declared a National Historic Landmark and a National Historic Mechanical and Civil Engineering Landmark.

Boathouse Row is the stretch of Victorian riverfront buildings upstream from the waterworks. They house the boats, called sculls, that amateur rowers use. American boat clubs were organized in the nineteenth century, and the first amateur sports association, Philadelphia's Schuylkill Navy, began in 1858. Member clubs staged their first official regatta on the Schuylkill in connection with the nation's centennial in 1876. Unless you know a member, you're unlikely to be invited inside, but the exterior views are delightfully memorable, day or night. When you're on Kelly Drive, the boathouses sit between you and the river, their stately stone-and-frame facades impressive and imposing. But the best view is from the West River Drive or the Schuylkill Expressway—unfortunately, you may not stop your car on these roads. (You can walk up the West River Drive from the Art Museum, though, and take photos until you run out of film.) All night long, the outlines of these houses are lit by thousands of small bulbs, shining brilliantly. Unforgettable.

The Mural Tour

*E*arly in 1999 Philadelphia sur-
passed Los Angeles as having the most
urban murals of any city in the country. On exhibit twenty-four hours a
day, with no admission fee and no
waiting lines, 2,000 murals tell the
story of the city's vitality, history, and
dreams. The brainchild of Jane Golden,
the Mural Arts Program has created
1,600 of those murals, inspiring hundreds of disadvantaged youths to work
with professional artists. To everyone's
pleasure, as the murals go up, graffiti
goes down. Here, with permission from
the Mural Arts Program, is a self-
guided tour of eleven popular murals.
By car, this tour takes about an hour.

- Start at the Tourist Center at
  Sixteenth Street and J. F. Kennedy
  Boulevard.

- Go west on Kennedy toward Twentieth Street, moving into the left lane
  as you drive.

- Turn left on Twentieth Street.

- In 1 block, turn right on Market
  Street.

- Continue $9/10$ mile, across the
  Schuylkill River. Turn right on
  Thirty-third Street.

- In $4/10$ mile, turn right on Hamilton
  Street.

- In 2 blocks, turn left on Thirty-first
  Street.

- In 1 block, turn left at Spring Garden Street. Look for Tuscan Landscape on your left.

- Get in left lane and turn left at
  light on Thirty-second Street
  (sign may be missing).

- In 4 blocks, turn right at Powelton
  Avenue. In $7/10$ mile, look across
  Fortieth Street for Boy with
  Raised Arm.

- Continue west on Powelton Avenue
  to third light, where it intersects with
  Market Street and Forty-fourth
  Street. Look across the intersection
  for A Celebration of Community.

- Turn left onto Market Street. Go
  $17/10$ miles, crossing Schuylkill
  River, and turn right on Twenty-
  third Street.

- In $6/10$ mile, cross South Street. Continue south, as Twenty-third Street
  bears right and becomes Grays
  Ferry Avenue.

- Go $7/10$ mile and turn left on
  Twenty-ninth Street.

- Go to second stop sign (Wharton
  Street) and look across intersection
  for Peace Wall.

- Continue on Twenty-ninth Street to
  second stop sign; turn left on Dickin-
  son Street. Go $13/10$ miles and turn
  left on Broad Street (which would be
  Fourteenth Street).

- At first light (Reed Street), look
  across intersection to see
  Mario Lanza.

- Continue on Broad Street about $8/10$
  mile; turn right on South Street.

- At Sixth Street, turn right and face
  Brazilian Rainforest.

- Continue on Sixth Street and turn
  right on Christian Street.

- Cross Seventh Street and look right
  for Moonlit Landscape.

The Mural Tour (continued)

- Continue on Christian Street and turn right on Ninth Street.

- Go 6 blocks and turn right on Pine Street.

- Turn left on Seventh Street, and stay on it for 1⁹/₁₀ miles. You will run into Washington Square. Follow Seventh clockwise around the square, staying in the right lane. At Race Street, bear left around Franklin Square. Stay on Seventh, in the middle lane. Go straight, driving under the multilane I–476 overpass.

- At Brown Street, look across intersection on left to see Immigration and the Dignity of Labor.

- Continue north on Seventh. Turn left at Poplar Street.

- Turn left on Eighth Street.

- In 2 blocks, turn right on Fairmount Avenue.

- Turn left on Twelfth Street.

- In 2 blocks, turn right on Mt. Vernon Street.

- In 1 block, turn sharp left on Ridge Avenue.

- In 1 block, at Green Street, look left to see Dr. J.

- Turn left on Green Street.

- Turn left on Eleventh Street.

- In 1 block, turn left on Mt. Vernon Street.

- When Mt. Vernon ends at Broad Street, turn left.

- Go 3 blocks to intersection of Spring Garden Street. Look across intersection on left for Common Threads

- Continue on Broad Street for 8 blocks to intersection with Vine Street. Look across intersection for A Tribute to the Family

- When Broad Street ends at City Hall, turn right onto J. F. Kennedy Boulevard. Go straight, crossing Fifteenth Street, to return to Tourist Center on your right.

Inner Suburbs

A scant block outside the city limits is the ***Barnes Foundation***, one of the finest private collections anywhere of French modern and post-Impressionist paintings. An extraordinary number of masterpieces by Renoir (180), Cézanne (69), and Matisse (60) provide the framework, with occasional gems by Picasso, Seurat, Modigliani, Degas, and others. The surrounding arboretum, rose garden, and lilacs make this place a special treat. The Barnes, well known but difficult to find, is located at 300 North Latchs Lane, Merion. It's open Thursday from 12:30 to 5:00 P.M. and Friday through Sunday from 9:30 A.M. to 5:00 P.M. Call (610) 667–0290 for driving directions and timed tickets.

Sometimes it books up months in advance. Adults pay $5.00 to enter—when they can get in.

Nearby **Harriton House** was the northernmost tobacco plantation operated on the slave economy. It's at 500 Harriton Road, Bryn Mawr. It's scheduled to be open 10:00 A.M. to 4:00 P.M., Wednesday through Saturday, but call ahead (610–525–0201).

Right in the middle of the beaten path is **Valley Forge National Historical Park** where George Washington and his 11,000 soldiers slept fitfully for the winter of 1777–78. If you are a history buff, an enthusiastic kid studying the Revolution, or just a healthy visitor out for a country walk—if you are, in fact, anything but a British loyalist—you'll enjoy the natural and historical beauty of the park.

If you want to walk in the woods while avoiding the crowds, drive a few miles north-northeast from Valley Forge to **Evansburg State Park**, where well-marked trails lead you through open fields and groves of tall evergreens—and few humans. Easiest access is from Germantown Pike between Collegeville and Fairview Village. Call (610) 489–3729 to reach the park office.

Not far away is the **Mill Grove Audubon Wildlife Sanctuary**, on a bluff overlooking the Perkiomen Creek. The museum features an array of the wildlife art of John James Audubon, in a rural setting with 3 miles of trails. The first American home of John James Audubon, the museum does not charge admission. It's open Tuesday through Saturday, 10:00 A.M. to 4:00 P.M., and Sunday 1:00 to 4:00 P.M. The grounds are open daily except Monday, from 7:00 A.M. to dusk. Find it at the intersection of Audubon Road and Pawlings Road, Audubon. Call (610) 666–5593 for details about naturalist programs, some of which are perfect for children.

Consider, too, scheduling a visit to the **Wharton Esherick Studio**. This Philadelphia-born artist spent much of his life in this curious, rustic five-story structure, creating designs mostly in wood. Like Barcelona's famed Antonio Gaudí (from whose name comes the word *gaudy*), Esherick eschewed straight lines and right angles. If you love the sensuality of delicately curved wooden forms, you'll flip. The two-story spiral staircase, carved from a single piece of wood, defies description but begs to be touched, as do many of the displayed pieces Esherick designed for the 1940 World's Fair in New York. Esherick, who died in

On the Beaten Path Attractions Worth Visiting

Academy of Music, Philadelphia

Independence Hall, Philadelphia

Liberty Bell, Philadelphia

Pennsylvania Academy of Fine Arts, Philadelphia

Rodin Museum, Philadelphia

Zoo in Philadelphia

State Capitol, Harrisburg

1970, shaped the copper sinks and forged the hinges. The studio, built over forty years, features oddly shaped scraps of patchworked wood on the floor and a cantilevered deck. The hour-long guided tour costs $5.00 and is not recommended for young children; leave one adult outside to run and climb with them in the woods. (Twenty years ago, the guide introduced herself as "Mr. Esherick's longtime companion," perhaps generating more questions than she answered.) Tours of this National Historic Landmark for Architecture are available March through December, 10:00 A.M. to 5:00 P.M. Saturday and 1:00 to 5:00 P.M. Sunday; groups midweek, by appointment. The studio is on the Horseshoe Trail near Country Club Road. Write to Box 595, Paoli, 19301; or call (610) 644–5822 for reservations and driving directions.

Art aficionados adore the **Brandywine River Museum** (Route 1, just south of Route 100, Chadds Ford), one of the largest and most comprehensive collections of works by N. C. Wyeth, Andrew Wyeth, Jamie Wyeth, and Howard Pyle. The exhibition changes often, so you might see your favorites (like Jamie's *Pig*) next to works you've never seen. It's open every day except Christmas, 9:30 A.M. to 4:00 P.M., and admission costs $5.00 for adults. Call (610) 388–2700 to check if the restaurant is open.

Any and every amateur and professional gardener—or wannabe—must stop at **Longwood Gardens** (Route 1, Kennett Square; mailing address, P.O. Box 501, 19348), where the extravagant, elegant, exquisite horticultural displays are open every day of the year from 9:00 A.M. to 5:00 P.M., staying open until 6:00 P.M. April through November. The conservatory opens at 10:00 A.M. Exotic flowers thrive in hothouses, and illuminated fountains highlight summer concerts. Longwood is a carnival of twenty indoor gardens, 400 performing-arts events each year, a gift shop, and a restaurant. Daily programs and classes enhance your gardening know-how. Admission costs $12.00 for adults ($8.00 on Tuesday). Call (610) 388–1000 for details.

Another landmark in Kennett Square features the polar opposite of Longwood's floral ecstasy. It's the **Mushroom Museum** (901 East Baltimore Pike [Route 1], Kennett Square), the only museum that fully explains the history, lore, and mystique of mushrooms. Movies, slides, and exhibits tell you more than you ever wanted to know about shiitake, portabella, and oyster mushrooms. The admission charge per adult is $1.25; gift shop entry is free. Call (610) 388–6082 for more details.

Trivia

Between 1896 and 1916, Siegmund Lubin produced more than 3,000 movies, built four studios, and manufactured and marketed film equipment. Today the Philadelphia optician is considered America's first movie mogul.

If you'd rather bike, walk, or skate than drive, try the **Schuylkill River Trail** to get from here to there. It extends 22 miles from Center City Philadelphia along the Schuylkill River to Valley Forge. (When completed, the trail will be 100 miles long.) If you live in the area, consider walking the trail in spurts till you cover it all.

Nothing could be farther off the beaten path than the **Museum of Mourning Art** at Arlington Cemetery in Drexel Hill (2900 State Road). Would you believe emblems of the skull and skeletons, hearses, and mourning jewelry in a museum? Call (610) 259–5800 to find out about hours, which are limited.

In Elkins Park, a northern suburb (take Route 611 north from the city), is Frank Lloyd Wright's only Jewish building: **Beth Sholom Congregation**. Dedicated in 1959, months after Wright's death, the building is a hexagonal pyramid of glass based, in part, on ideas put forth by the synagogue's distinguished and forward-looking rabbi, Mortimer Cohen. The building was intended to be self-contained and to stand apart from its suburban surroundings. It succeeds. Wright designed the fittings, too: the lighting, the seating, and the placement of the religious symbols. When the Museum of the Diaspora in Tel Aviv, Israel, recently created a permanent exhibit of synagogues to represent eighteen centuries of Judaism, it chose Beth Sholom for the Twentieth Century. Tours of the sanctuary, at Old York Road and Foxcroft Road, are Sunday through Wednesday by appointment only, or you may attend religious services. Call (215) 887–1342.

Pennsylvania Dutch Country: Plain and Fancy

About 300 years ago, groups of religious refugees from the Rhine region of Germany migrated to southeastern Pennsylvania. These settlers, mostly peasant farmers, came to take advantage of the religious freedom offered by William Penn. They included Amish and Mennonites—people of "plain" dress—and Lutherans and other Reformed groups of more worldly attire, sometimes called "fancy." Over time, these people became known as "Pennsylvania Dutch," with the *Dutch* really a misinterpretation of the original *Deutsch*.

Wilkum to Lancaster County and the scenic Pennsylvania Dutch Country, where life moves at a slower pace and centers around time-honored traditions and values. Here you find beautiful scenery punctuated with one-room schoolhouses and wooden covered bridges, modern farm machinery pulled by mules, homemade clothing and quilts hanging to dry. You hear the clip-clop of horses' hooves on quiet country roads. The plain folks are less materialistic and less hurried than their urban counterparts, yet the highways through Lancaster County have grown touristy, as various people attempt to capitalize on the otherworldliness of these self-effacing settlers. Virtually any T-shirt shop, quilt boutique, or restaurant in the area can hand you a brochure with a self-guided driving tour. For a glimpse of a real Pennsylvania Dutch family, enjoy the movie *Witness* and leave these people alone.

At the **Landis Valley Museum** north of Lancaster, you can see eighteen historic buildings filled with the arts and crafts, tools and tales of German immigrants. It's open from March through November, Monday to Saturday 9:00 A.M. to 5:00 P.M. and Sunday noon to 5:00 P.M., with hour-long guided tours and special programs every Sunday. From downtown Lancaster, take Route 272 north to 2451 Kissel Hill Road. For more details call (717) 569–0401.

The City of Lancaster served as the capital of the United States for almost an entire day. It was September 27, 1777, and British invaders were threatening the capital in Philadelphia. The Continental Congress and the Executive Council of Pennsylvania fled to Lancaster, where they held one session of congress. Believing that the British were in hot pursuit, congress moved across the Susquehanna River to York. Find out

---

Verna Steck's Dutch Shoofly Pie

*C*rumb together:

1 cup flour

²/₃ cup brown sugar

1 rounded tablespoon shortening

¹/₂ teaspoon cinnamon

Reserve ¹/₂ cup for top.

Mix:

1 beaten egg

1 cup King syrup

1 cup boiling water

1 teaspoon baking soda

Add crumbs to this mix. Stir until moistened. Pour into unbaked dough shell and top with ¹/₂ cup crumbs. Bake at 350 degrees for 30 to 40 minutes.

Merriam Webster *defines a "shoofly" as either a child's rocker that resembles an animal figure or a plant that is believed to repel flies. Shoofly pie, it says, is a rich pie of Pennsylvania-Dutch origin; the word first appeared in 1926.*

more at the ***Discover Lancaster County History Museum*** (2249 Route 30 East, Lancaster). The museum opens daily at 9:00 A.M. and charges $6.00 per adult; since closing time varies, you may want to call (717) 393–3679 to find out.

In western and southern Lancaster County, the hills are more pronounced, and the views more dramatic. Along the Susquehanna River you'll find many scenic overlooks that offer breathtaking views of the river far below.

Lancaster County features one of the largest concentrations of antiques in the country. In Adamstown, the "Sunday Antiques Capital of the United States," over 7,000 antique dealers gather to display and sell their merchandise. Every Sunday from 7:30 A.M. until 4:00 P.M., Adamstown (www.antiquescapital.com) becomes the essential antiquers' paradise. Dozens of shops line Route 272, with ***Renninger's*** (www.renningers. com) one of the best known and best loved. If you crave memories from any bygone era—even the 1990s—here's where to find what you're looking for. Take the Pennsylvania Turnpike to exit 21, then north on Route 272.

Since 1875, ***Groff's Meats*** has been selling wholesale and retail meat in Elizabethtown. The fourth generation of Groffs—two brothers and two sisters—now run the business. Groff relatives and employees buy and

Recipe for Mincemeat Drops from Groff's Meats

*I*ngredients:

2 cups flour

¹/₂ teaspoon salt

¹/₂ teaspoon baking soda

¹/₂ cup shortening, soft

1 cup packed brown sugar

1 egg

¹/₂ cup milk

¹/₂ cup Groff's moist mincemeat

1¹/₂ cups rolled oatmeal (instant or old-fashioned)

Sift together flour, salt, and baking soda into bowl. Add shortening, sugar, egg, and milk, and beat until smooth. Drop by the teaspoonful on a greased and floured cookie sheet. Bake at 375 degrees for 12 to 15 minutes.

Optional frosting:

2 tablespoons butter

3 cups icing sugar

3 tablespoons milk

¹/₄ teaspoon maple flavoring

slaughter cattle and pigs, then lovingly and painstakingly convert them into hams, bacon, and sweet bologna, and, in the fall, mincemeat: a super-secret family recipe of beef and suet, local apples, raisins, sherry wine, rum concentrate, and spices. "Making mincemeat takes a while," says Joseph Groff. "On Saturday we cook our raisins. On Tuesday we peel and core fresh local apples. On Thursday we put it all together for mincemeat." Since the Groffs use only healthy, wholesome, free-range raisins, no minces are killed to make this concoction. Groff's Meats makes five and a half tons—*tons*—of mincemeat a week during mincemeat season, which coincides roughly with autumn leaves. (If storage space fills up, they might skip a week.) Visit Groff's Meats at 33 North Market Street, Elizabeth-town, or place a 2-pound or 35-pound order by calling (717) 367–1246.

You want corn chips? You want onion rings? **Herr Foods** is the third-largest snack-food company in the country, employing a thousand peo-ple and distributing its munchies in ten northeastern states. The factory tour includes a twenty-five-minute video (great for kids). Then you walk through windowed corridors, watching people and machines washing, peeling, slicing, cooking, and seasoning the potatoes—then bagging, boxing, and preparing them for shipment. Drool no more. Reach onto the conveyor belt and pick up a free handful of fresh, warm chips. Yum. Back in the visitors center, you get a free packaged snack and the chance to buy anything else remotely corn-chip related. Herr's is at the intersec-tion of Herr Drive and Route 272 in Nottingham, just south of Lancaster. The visitors center is open weekdays year-round except for major holi-days, 8:00 A.M. to 5:00 P.M. Monday through Thursday; it closes an hour earlier on Friday. The free hour-long tour runs on the hour from 9:00 A.M. to 3:00 P.M. Monday through Thursday, 9:00 to 11:00 A.M. on Friday. Call ahead (800–637–6225) for reservations, especially in summer.

Visit the demonstration garden and see the agricultural experiments taking place at the **Rodale Institute.** Rodale, which publishes *Preven-tion* and other magazines, welcomes visitors from May through November, Monday through Saturday 9:00 A.M. to 5:00 P.M. and Sun-day noon to 5:00 P.M. The tour lasts about ninety minutes. Call (610) 683–6383 or (610) 683–1400.

Reading

People in the East know Reading for its outlets, its Pennsylvania Dutch heritage, and its antiques marts. But few people recognize that in some ways, Reading *is* the East—the East as in Orient, China, and pagodas. At the top of Mt. Penn, the seven-story **Pagoda** dominates the town's skyline. In the early 1900s William Abbott Witman bought this land to quarry its stone. But the quarrying operation defaced the mountain, which he hid by building, of all things, a pagoda, which he hoped would become a luxury hotel. When Witman's license to serve alcohol was denied, the building fell into the hands of a bank. In 1910 an investor bought the whole shebang, then sold it to the City of Reading for a dollar. You can visit, free, Friday to Tuesday, noon to 4:00 P.M. A gift shop is on the fourth level. To get there, start in Reading and drive uphill. For precise driving directions call (610) 375–6399 during open hours.

Birds: more than enough to impress Sir Alfred Hitchcock but not enough to scare anyone. To see them, visit **Hawk Mountain Sanctuary,** 2,400 acres of natural habitat in the Kittatinny *(kitta tinny)* Ridge, designed to foster the conservation of birds of prey and other wildlife. Before the sanctuary was created in 1934, hunters freely shot migrating raptors— hawks, eagles, ospreys, and falcons—that flew over Hawk Mountain each fall. Now the birds are safe. No matter which of the 365 days of the year you choose to visit, you'll see birds. About 18,000 raptors plus a thousand humans visit on a mild October weekend day. In spring warblers and other songbirds visit. In June, when the mountain laurels bloom, nesting birds sing. In winter you can see ruffed grouse in the forest and wintering finches and sparrows near the bird feeders at the visitor's center. Trails are open dawn to dusk; adults pay $4.00 to enter, $6.00 on autumn weekends. From Route I–78, take the Hamburg exit. Drive north on Route 61, then veer right to go north on Route 895. Turn right at Drehersville. You can write to the Hawk Mountain Sanctuary, Hawk Mountain Road, Route 2, Kempton, 19529, or call (610) 756–6961.

Where's Joe's?

*M*y husband and I usually celebrate our wedding anniversary by quitting work at noon, taking a walk in the woods, and enjoying a special dinner. One year we were aiming for Joe's, a then-famous (now shuttered) restaurant in Reading that served mushrooms: mushroom soup, sautéed mushrooms, mushroom ice cream. We drove to Reading but couldn't find Joe's, so we asked for directions.

Six people tried to help. "Hmmm," they said. "Joe's. Not easy to get there from here." Or, "I'm not sure, really." Or, "Joe's. Hmm." We arrived thirty minutes late for shiitake bisque, which was excellent. Whenever we get lost in a small town and people don't seem to be able to give us directions to their next-door neighbor's house, we tease each other, "Know how to get to Joe's?"

Daniel Boone Homestead

Daniel Boone, the legendary pioneer, was born and raised in Birdsboro. You can visit the **Daniel Boone Homestead** (mailing address: R.D. 2, Box 162, Birdsboro 19508) and learn about the lifestyles of different cultures in the eighteenth century in rural Pennsylvania. From Reading, take Route 422 east. Scheduled hours are Tuesday through Saturday 9:00 A.M. to 5:00 P.M., and Sunday noon to 5:00 P.M. The homestead is closed Monday except for Memorial Day and on July 4 and Labor Day; hours may change, so call (215) 582–4900 to check.

Capital District

Harrisburg, the state capital, borders the Susquehanna River and features quite a scenic waterfront for an inland city. The State Capitol, dedicated by Theodore Roosevelt, has a dome modeled after St. Peter's Basilica in Rome and a staircase that emulates the Opera of Paris. City Island, refashioned in the late 1980s, has recreational opportunities to suit many tastes. You can get there by car, bike, or on foot on the Walnut Street Bridge.

While you're in the vicinity, try dinner at **Alfred's Victorian**, a pleasant place in Middletown where the house specialty is the Flaming Victorian Salad, which the server makes with flourish and pizzazz at your tableside. The best seats at Alfred's are at the two round tables in the turret:

Table Nine downstairs, Table Thirty-two upstairs. The address is 38 North Union Street. To make reservations or order a cookbook call (717) 944–4929.

A short drive down I–83 from Harrisburg brings you to York, a biggish town (or a smallish city) whose history is everywhere. Everywhere in downtown, that is. You can see the town's heritage in larger-than-life murals throughout the downtown district.

Light Up Your Life

*M*iddletown is the home of the nuclear power plant called **Three Mile Island (TMI),** *where a near-catastrophe occurred in March 1979. If you can't have a flaming salad in the shadow of a nuclear tower, where can you? So after a sinful peanut butter pie, we head to TMI. The guard stops us unceremoniously. "May I help you?" he asks. "I want to get on the Turnpike, heading west." "So get on," he says, not offering driving directions. Is he for real? I turn around, retrace my route, and ask someone else.*

While that's one way to put a fire in someone's belly, a more pleasant alternative is to try making the Flaming Victorian Salad, served at Alfred's Victorian in Middletown, at home.

1/2 teaspoon salt

1 clove garlic

1 tablespoon Worcestershire sauce

dash hot sauce

1 tablespoon egg substitute

2-3 tablespoons olive oil

1 teaspoon lemon juice

1/4 cup celery, chopped

1/4 cup almonds, sliced

1/4 cup bacon bits

1/4 cup raisins

5 ounces romaine lettuce

3 ounces spinach

1-2 tablespoons Parmesan cheese

fresh ground black pepper

croutons

brandy

triple sec

Sprinkle salt into an oversized, wooden salad bowl. Rub the garlic clove around the bowl, creating a fine scent and garlic salt. Pour on the Worcestershire sauce, the hot sauce, the egg substitute, the olive oil, and the lemon juice. Add celery, almonds, bacon bits and raisins. Blend these ingredients. Add romaine lettuce and spinach; sprinkle Parmesan cheese and pepper on top. Make a nest in the center of the greens, filling it with croutons. Mix one part brandy with two parts triple sec and heat—over a tableside cooktop, if you have such. Let the alcohol catch fire, then pour it over the croutons from an altitude as high as you can reach. Stir the salad while the croutons blaze. Toss again and serve.

Herskey Kiss Lamppost

Hersheypark may be too crowded for you, but consider *Chocolate World* at the entrance to Hersheypark, in Hershey, where all the world's sweet. A nine-minute ride takes you through a simulated chocolate factory. It's interesting for adults and a treat for kids, and it's open from 9:00 A.M. to 5:00 P.M. every day but Christmas. Call (717) 534–4900 or (800) 437–7439. You can't beat the price (it's free), and you get free candy treats at the end.

If you like strummin' on the ole banjo, visit the *Martin Guitar Company*, Northampton, and take a free, one-hour guided tour of the manufacture of guitars and guitar strings. The tour starts weekdays at 1:15 P.M., and children must be at least twelve to attend. The factory, museum, and shop are at 510 Sycamore Street. Call (610) 759–2837 for more details.

Unique Shopping Experiences

Anything you want to buy, you can find in Southeastern Pennsylvania, except, perhaps, an I ♥ NY button or a replica of the Eiffel Tower. Some specialized emporia stand out from the crowd. Ready. Set. Shop.

Baldwin's Book Barn (865 Lenape Road, West Chester, in the Brandywine Valley) has been buying and selling rare and used books since 1934. Visitors spend hours browsing an inventory of 400,000 volumes arranged on five floors of an 1822 barn. Beyond the potbellied stove

Kisses for Anne

and antique furnishings, Baldwin's runs a covert global operation: an Internet catalog department, reaching avid collectors (www.bookbarn. com). Call (610) 696-0816 or (888) 901-8822. Hours are weekdays 9:00 A.M. to 9:00 P.M. and weekends 10:00 A.M. to 5:00 P.M.

For the young and the young-at-heart, try one of the eight Southeastern Pennsylvania locations of *Zany Brainy*, a toy store with intelligence. Books and bears, of course, but also crafts and capacious caprice, plus clever employees. The founder, David Schlessinger, created Encore, a successful chain of discount book stores, with his bar mitzvah gifts. He sold the book stores, started the toy stores. He's zany and brainy. Go to www.zanybrainy.com or call (610) 642-4050 to access jigsaw puzzles, craft supplies, and store hours.

If it's music you want—or a T-shirt, poster, or wine cork thereof—visit the tiny *Philadelphia Orchestra Gift Shop* (1420 Locust Street, Philadelphia). It's open daily except Sunday, 11:00 A.M. to 5:00 P.M., staying open until 8:00 P.M. on concert evenings. Call (215) 893-1952 to see if the conductors-as-hand-puppets are still available.

Kitchen Kettle Village (Route 340, Old Philadelphia Pike, Intercourse, about 10 miles east of Lancaster) sells sixty varieties of all-natural jams and jellies. It's open year-round, 9:00 A.M. to 5:00 P.M.; closed Sunday. Call (800) 732-3538 or (717) 768-8261 for details.

Many Amish quilts are passed down from generation to generation as family heirlooms, and in the Lancaster area you can find hundreds of handmade quilts. *Better Homes and Gardens* called the *Old Country Store* (Route 340, Old Philadelphia Pike, Intercourse) one of the ten best quilt shops in America: top-quality handsewn quilts, pillows, cornhusk bunnies, and more, plus fabric so that you can make some yourself. Upstairs is a quilt museum. It's open Monday through Saturday 9:00 A.M. to 5:00 P.M.,

The Secret's Out

Central PA *magazine calls it the worst-kept cold-war-era secret. It's Site R, built in the early 1950s as a relocation site for the Pentagon in case of nuclear war. It's supposed to be a secret, but the chain-link fences topped with barbed wire and the tall antennae lighting the sky at night hint strongly that something is going on. In the area of Raven Rock Mountain, in the southwest corner of Adams County, keep your eyes peeled for a buried bunker.*

November through May, and until 8:00 P.M. the rest of the year. Call (800) 828–8218 or (717) 768–7101.

On South Street in Philadelphia, the street of song, teens and young adults hang out. To see spiked orange hair, go to South Street. To find black leather pants and wristlets, go to South Street. To find unique clothing, exotic jewelry, and crafts made in Mexico and points south, go to *Eye's Gallery* (402 South Street; 215–925–0193). Owner Julia Zagar has an eye for style—plus an artist-husband whose all-ceramic tile murals grace other blocks of South Street.

The *Italian Market* is not a store, it's a life. Sprawled on both sides of South Ninth Street, between Catherine Street and Washington Avenue, and spilling over onto most of the cross streets, too, it is an open-air market where you can pick up every foodstuff known to Italians or Italian-Americans. You want cheese? Try DiBruno Brothers (930 South Ninth Street). You want sausage? Try Fiorella Brothers (817 Christian Street). You want cannoli (everybody wants cannoli)? Try Termini (1523 South Eighth Street). Meanwhile, in the stores behind the stands, you can buy sofas, socks, and sandwiches. Open every day but Sunday. Have a blast—or a baloney.

In 1974 the Puerto Rican community created *Taller Puertorriqueño* to preserve, develop, and promote Puerto Rican art and culture and to support a better understanding of other Latin American cultures. The bookstore and gallery (2721 North Fifth Street; 215–426–3311) sell music, children's books, jewelry, poetry, T-shirts, and more in English and Spanish.

If you're lost, or planning to be lost, you can find virtually any map, globe, or atlas at *Franklin Maps* (333 South Henderson Road, King of Prussia). It has an amazing array of topographic maps, nautical charts, hiking and canoeing guides, even some antique maps. Call (610) 265–6277 or (800) 356–8676 for details. Store hours are 8:30 A.M. to 5:00 P.M. weekdays, and it opens at 11:00 A.M. on Saturday.

Material Culture (4700 Wissahickon Avenue, Philadelphia) collects furniture, rugs, and artifacts from all over the world so that you can collect them and take them home without hassling customs officials. You can find Chinese ceremonial coffers, Afghan prayer rugs, and hand-painted barber-shop signs from Ghana, and they all, somehow, look as though they belong together. The industrial building feels like an outdoor bazaar in a foreign locale—yet here it is, in a commercial district just off a six-lane highway in America. Call (215) 849–8030 for driving directions, or visit the store on the Web at www.materialculture.com.

Material Culture is open Sunday from noon to 5:00 P.M. and all other days from 10:00 A.M. to 6:00 P.M.

One of the old-world traditions that followed the Pennsylvania Dutch include the large, colorful geometric patterns—called hex signs—used to decorate barns. Mystical bird and floral designs graced birth and marriage certificates, family bibles, and some furniture. Popular symbols included sun wheels for warmth and fertility, hearts for love, birds (called Distelfinks) for good luck and happiness, tulips for faith, and stars for luck. Red signified emotions, yellow meant love of people and the sun, green represented growing things, blue meant protection, white symbolized purity, and brown stood for mother earth. Find an extensive collection at *Will-Char, The Hex Place* (3056 Route 30, East Paradise, 717–687–8329; e-mail hexsigns@desupernet.net).

Best Annual Events in Southeastern Pennsylvania

- Wake up early on New Year's Day and catch the *Mummers Parade*, the all-Philadelphia strut of 30,000 spectacularly costumed "Mummers." Stand anywhere on South Broad Street or call (215) 636–1666 to find about tickets for the wrap-up ceremonies in the Pennsylvania Convention Center.

- In Philadelphia, *Valentine's Day* is for lovers of jazz. A nine-day festival has more than ninety musical events at spots around town, many of which are free. Call (215) 636–1666 for details.

- Spring means flowers, but nowhere more so than in Philadelphia. At the *Philadelphia Flower Show*—the largest and most prestigious flower show in the world—ten acres of lush gardens and lavish floral settings inspire gardeners of all varieties. It's held early in March at the Pennsylvania Convention Center. There's an admission fee, paid even by the show's judges. Call the Pennsylvania Horticultural Society at (215) 988–8800 for dates and details.

- During March, Philadelphia runs the *Book and Cook Festival*, inviting cookbook authors from around the country to pair up with restaurants and create special meals. The event began in 1985, and by 1999 ninety authors showed up, paired with restaurateurs, and showed off their prowess. Call (215) 636–1666 for details.

- Mid April, at the *Philadelphia Antiques Show*, some of the nation's finest merchants of antique furnishings bring their wares to the 103RD Engineers Armory, Thirty-third Street, Philadelphia. Proceeds benefit the University of Pennsylvania Medical Center. Tickets cost $12 per adult, $20 for a guided tour. For more details visit www.philaantiques.com, or call (215) 387–3500.

- Late April, *Pridefest Philadelphia* is a comprehensive annual gay and lesbian symposium and festival, held at various sites. Call (215) 732–3378.

- The *Devon Horse Show and Country Fair*, the nation's largest outdoor horse show, creates traffic jams up and down

Route 30 along the historic Main Line for a week at the end of May. It's at the **Devon Fairgrounds**, which you can reach at (610) 964–0550.

- First weekend in June celebrates wheels in Philadelphia: two wheels, not four. It's the **First Union U.S./Pro Cycling Championship**, the nation's largest one-day professional cycling event. Call (215) 636–1666 for the route and the times. Stake out a spot and cheer for your favorite rider.

- Initiated in 1950 to preserve traditions and customs, the **Kutztown Pennsylvania Dutch Festival** celebrates the anachronistic lifestyles of the Amish, Mennonite, and Brethren people in an annual nine-day exposition. Special pageants show traditional Amish weddings and barn raisings, although the Amish don't actually participate, due to religious constraints. Locals demonstrate sheep-shearing, ironworking, and quilting. Watch ethnic dances with 110,000 other people. Taste old-world foods like bratwurst and shoofly pie. Scheduled in late June/early July, the festival has moved to the Schuylkill County Fairgrounds in Summit Station, which you can reach from exit 7 or exit 9 off I–78 or from exit 31 off I–81. Because of the popularity of the event, hotels, bed-and-breakfasts, and campgrounds fill up quickly, so reserve early. Contact the festival at 461 Vine Lane, Summit Station, 17979, or call (610) 683–8707 or (800) 765–7282.

- The **Philadelphia Folk Festival** is three days of traditional and contemporary folk music, dance, crafts, camping, campfire sings, storytelling, juggling, and special children's activities. A family-oriented event, the festival takes place on the Old Pool Farm near Schwenksville, in Montgomery County, the last weekend in August. You can camp for the weekend or spend a day. Parking is available on the site, and children under age twelve are admitted free to all concert events. For tickets and information call (215) 242–0150 or (800) 556–3655.

- Her Majesty is waiting for you at the **Renaissance Faire**, weekends from late August through mid-October. Watch blacksmiths, taste "roasted turkey legges," and let storytellers mesmerize your children. Chart your course to Victorian Mount Hope Estate and Winery, Route 72, $1/2$ mile south of Pennsylvania Turnpike exit 20 (mailing address, Box 685, Cornwall, 17016; Web site, www.parenaissancefaire.com; phone, (717) 665–7021).

- At **Hersheypark** you can celebrate the Jewish Festival of Sukkot, which occurs in late September or early October. The all-Kosher event features hot dogs, potato knishes, and more, plus a day of rides to celebrate the harvest season. For details call the **Central Pennsylvania Kosher Mart** (which operates a Glatt Kosher stand at Hersheypark all season) at (717) 392–5111. Sukkot proceeds go to the local Mikveh, a Jewish charity.

- The **Historical Society of the Cocalico Valley** holds its antiques show every October. Call The Artworks at Doneckers, a four-story, one-of-a-kind shopping situation in a former shoe factory, (717) 738–9503 for details.

- Sometime in the fall, shortly before your holiday shopping frenzy peaks, it's time for the **Philadelphia Museum of Art Craft Show** (Pennsylvania Convention Center, Twelfth and Arch Streets), one of the premiere juried craft shows in the country. Started in 1976, the show benefits the art museum—and you, if you shop for jewelry, hand-made paper, rocking chairs, candles, custom-fitted boots, and more. Phone (215) 684–7931 for exact dates.

PLACES TO STAY IN SOUTH-EASTERN PENNSYLVANIA

EPHRATA
Inns at Doneckers,
318 North State Street and
301 West Main Street;
(717) 738–9502.

KEMPTON
Hawk Mountain Bed &
Breakfast, 221 Stony Run
Valley Road;
(610) 756–4224.

LAMPETER
Australian Walkabout Inn
Bed & Breakfast,
837 Village Road;
(717) 464–0707.

LIMA
Hamanassett Bed and
Breakfast, P.O. Box 129,
Lima 19037;
(610) 459–3000. Two-night
minimum.

PHILADELPHIA
Uncle's Upstairs Inn,
1220 Locust Street;
(215) 546–6660;
fax (215) 546–1653.

PLACES TO EAT IN SOUTH-EASTERN PENNSYLVANIA

DENVER
Zinn's Diner, Route 272,
just north of exit 21 on the
Pennsylvania Turnpike;
(717) 336–2210. While

waiting for your wet-
bottom shoofly pie, read
the placemat, which tells
you mileage to nearby
communities.

EASTON
Pearly Baker's Ale House,
11 Centre Square;
(610) 253–9949.

Tea Room, 208 Spring
Garden Street;
(610) 515–1154. Shops plus
food and drink.

KINTNERSVILLE
Great American Grille,
Route 611 and Route 32;
(610) 847–2023. Free pop-
corn before (or after) you're
served. Crayons available
(walls are decorated with
art created by waiting
patrons). To promote AIDS
awareness, free condoms
are offered at the bar. Open
daily Memorial Day to
Labor Day; Wednesday
through Sunday the rest of
the year; lunch and dinner.

MIDDLETOWN
Alfred's Victorian, 38 North
Union; (717) 944–5373.
Specialty: Flaming
Victorian Salad.

PHILADELPHIA
BLT's Cobblefish,
443 Shurs Lane (in the
Manayunk section);
(215) 483–5478.

Dante & Luigi's, Tenth and
Catherine Streets, South
Philadelphia; (215)
922–9501. The oldest Italian restaurant in America.

DiNardo's, 312 Race Street;
(215) 925–5515. Best
known for hardshell crabs.

Jim's Steaks, 400 South
Street; (215) 928–1911.
Cheesesteaks and hoagies.

Lena, 246 Market Street;
(215) 625–4888. Look at
pictures of desserts
through a stereopticon
while your server
describes them.

Liberties, 705 North
Second Street;
(215) 238–0660. Check out
the store next door, with
more antique footed tubs
than you can count, old
British pub interiors, and
stunning stained glass—
just what you need to
redecorate your home.

Pat's King of Steaks,
1237 East Passyunk
Avenue; (215) 468–1546.
Cheesesteaks and hoagies.

Tavern on Green, Twenty-
first and Green Streets;
(215) 235–6767.

Valley Green Inn, Spring-
field Avenue and
Wissahickon Creek;
(215) 247–1730. An ancient
(built in 1850, sits on the
site of an establishment
that existed in the 1770s)
hostelry serving superb
food.

Villa di Roma,
936 Ninth Street;
(215) 592–1295. Italian
food with gravy (don't *ever*
call it "tomato sauce") in a
cheesy, tacky, brightly lit
setting. Short, cylindrical
wine glasses and waitresses
who call you "Hon."

READING
Antique Airplane
Restaurant and Lounge,
4635 Perkiomen Avenue,
Route 422 East;
(610) 779–2345.

WEST CHESTER
Dilworthtown Inn,
1390 Old Wilmington Pike;
(610) 399–1390 or
www.dilworthtown.com.
Dinner only.

Trivia

*You can probably buy
Philadelphia-style cheesesteaks in Paris, Maine;
Paris, Texas; or Paris, Kentucky. But to get the real
thing, you have to go to
Philadelphia—where the
rolls originate in Atlantic
City, New Jersey. We're talking eating here, not dining.
According to local cheesesteak expert Joel Perloff,
"You have to look real hard
to find a bad cheesesteak in
Philadelphia."*

South Central Pennsylvania: Valleys of the Susquehanna

It's kooky, it's curvy, it's the **Horseshoe Curve,** and it's a great place to start visiting South Central Pennsylvania. As the early railroads expanded westward, the Pennsylvania Railroad ran into a major snag at Altoona: mountains. The grade in the Alleghenies was far too steep for a run straight up or down. To circumvent the situation and to connect two sides of Kittanning Point, engineers designed a huge, bending track, which opened to train traffic in 1854. Men used picks, shovels, and horses to carve the curve, which is still considered an engineering marvel, to say nothing of a tourist's paradise. The length of the curve is 2,375 feet; the grade is 1.8 percent; the degree of curvature is 9 degrees, 25 minutes; and the central angle is 220 degrees.

When you come to this spot where trains make a U-turn, ride the funicular or walk the 194 steps to the top; a sturdy fence protects your body from the trains but leaves your eyes and ears free to enjoy. To imagine what it's like, think of a football stadium fifty times larger than reality. You are sitting at the end near the goalpost, two rows down from the top tier. At the topmost level of the stadium, a train approaches from the far end. It chugs on by, wrapping around the curve—and around you—as the engineer waves and toots his whistle. The long train continues on the other side of the stadium so that at one point, you are surrounded by an endless iron snake. Eventually it disappears around another curve, but you can still hear it, and everyone near you is still smiling. If the weather's nice, you can have a picnic while waiting for a few more of the sixty passenger and freight trains that traverse the curve daily. Visiting hours are 9:30 A.M. to 7:00 P.M. daily, April through October; and 10:00 A.M. to 4:30 P.M. except Monday, November through April. It closes from the first Sunday in January through March. For $3.50 you can visit the curve

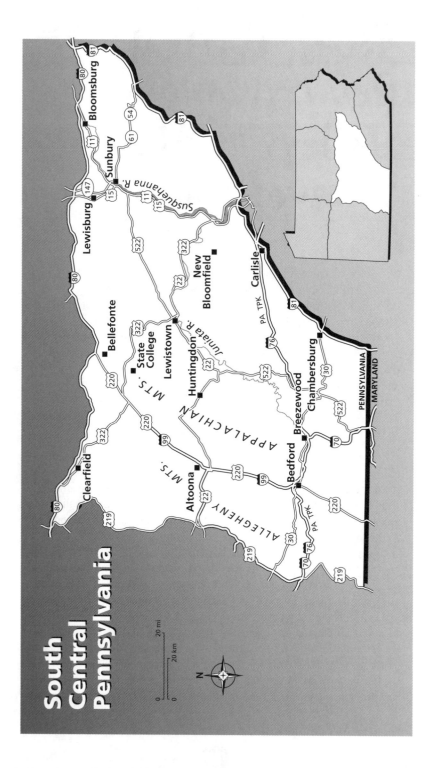

AUTHOR'S TOP TEN FAVORITES IN
SOUTH CENTRAL PENNSYLVANIA

Apple orchards

Bellefonte

Church on the Turnpike

Coffee Pot

Eisenhower National Historic Site

Horseshoe Curve

Leap the Dips

Millersburg Ferry

Slinky Store

Utz Potato Chips

and ride the funicular railway round-trip. Check out the Web site at www.railroadcity.com.

If this is your first visit to the area, you might choose to start at the **Railroaders Memorial Museum**, at 1300 Ninth Avenue, Altoona (814– 946–0834 or rrcity@aol.com) to understand this engineering marvel–turned–National Historic Landmark. To get to the museum from I–99, take the Seventeenth Street exit, then turn right on Ninth Avenue. Admission to the museum costs $8.50 per adult. It's open year-round from 10:00 A.M. to 5:00 P.M.; closed Monday between November and April.

It costs only $2.50 to ride **Leap the Dips**, the historic, wooden side-friction roller coaster in Altoona's **Lakemont Park**. The amusement reopened in 1999 after fourteen years in mothballs; the Leap the Dips Foundation spent a million bucks restoring the original cars and replacing the superstructure. If you have an extra half-million dollars to donate to this National Historic Landmark, mail a check to the Foundation, 700 Park Avenue, Altoona 16601, or call (814) 949–7275. Your donation is tax deductible. To get there from I–80, take Route 220 south; after Route 220 becomes I–99, exit at Frankstown Road. Or visit www.leapthedips.org.

You'll find another historic landmark at 3205 Sixth Avenue. **Reighard's** claims to be America's oldest gasoline station, offering full service to motorists since 1909.

Just 12 miles west of Altoona on Route 22, visit the **Allegheny Portage Railroad**, now a National Historic Site. At this place in 1834, canal boats were loaded onto rail cars, reducing the trip between Philadelphia and Pittsburgh from three weeks by wagon to four days by railroad and canal. At the visitors center you can take a brief history lesson. You can walk forested trails along the railroad's route, or if you're so inclined, watch a costumed stonecutting demonstration. It's open from 9:00 A.M. to 6:00 P.M. from Memorial Day to Labor Day, closing an hour earlier the rest of the year; closed Christmas day. For more information write Allegheny Portage Railroad, Box 189, Cresson 16630, or call (814) 886–6150.

If you head north on Route 220, then north on Route 360 and west on Route 322, you come to Clearfield, which originated as the Indian town of Chinklacamoose. A portion of the Old Town Historic District is listed on the National Register of Historic Places. Several stately Victorian homes offer an interesting self-guided walking tour extending 4 blocks along Front Street.

West of Altoona, along Route 22, visit the *Mt. Assisi Monastery* and the *Holy House of Father Gallitzin* in Loretto. Father Gallitzin was a Russian prince who gave up his title and inheritance; he became the first priest to receive all the orders in the United States, and he served the community of Loretto. Catholics on a pilgrimage find it refreshing to stop there as well as at the Carmelite Monastery and St. Michael's Church. For more information, and to schedule a visit, call (814) 472–9483, or write the Prince Gallitzin Chapel House, P.O. Box 87, Loretto, 15940.

Heading southeast from Altoona, you discover the town of State College, home of Pennsylvania State University (not to be confused with the University of Pennsylvania, which is in Philadelphia). It's a member of the Big Ten football conference, so sports—playing, watching, and wearing blue-and-white outfits—is an important undergraduate major. Penn State was founded in 1855 as the Farmers' High School. It has grown. Beaver Stadium, the fourth-largest stadium in the country, is often packed beyond its 93,967–seat capacity.

Valleys of the Susquehanna

Due north of State College, although there are no direct roads, is Bellefonte, meaning beautiful fountain. It's best known for its *Big Spring*, which gushes 11.5 million gallons of water each day. This diminutive town bred seven governors of Pennsylvania. How small a town is Bellefonte? Small enough that when the author, age eleven,

How Cows Teach Gin Rummy

If you do it right, watching cows can teach you to be an expert gin-rummy player. How? Ask Charlie Claycomb, now of San Diego, originally from Williamsburg, a rural community near Altoona.

"When you're seven," says Claycomb, "the first job they give you on a farm is watching cows. There are no fences, and you have to watch the cows to make sure they don't wander into the alfalfa patch, because alfalfa makes the milk go sour."

Watching cows, though, is not a full-time occupation. To keep busy Claycomb played 500-rummy nonstop with his neighbor, Jerry Michelone, another seven-year-old cow watcher.

Years of practice made Claycomb the best gin-rummy player at the deluxe La Costa Country Club in Southern California. And he owes it all, he says, to watching cows in Pennsylvania.

Trivia

Some say the towns named Paint and Scalp Level hint at the area's Indian heritage. Others say a man wanted his land cleared real low—to scalp level, he told the workmen. Choose the etymology you prefer.

traveled here alone by train, the society column of the *Centre Daily Times* reported her visit.

Boalsburg is home to the **Pennsylvania Military Museum**, honoring the women and men of Pennsylvania who served their country in war. From Benjamin Franklin's first military unit—the Associators—through the conflict in Viet Nam, this museum tells the tale. A highlight is the recreated World War I battlefield, complete with sound and lighting effects. The museum, which charges admission, is open Tuesday through Saturday from 9:00 A.M. to 5:00 P.M.; Sunday from noon to 5:00 P.M.; closed Mondays and holidays except Memorial Day, July 4, and Labor Day. For more details write to Box 148, Boalsburg 16827, or call (814) 466-6263.

If you think Christopher Columbus sailed up the Susquehanna River on his second voyage, you're wrong. Nonetheless some of the Spanish explorer's relics and heirlooms are on exhibit at the **Boal Mansion and Columbus Chapel,** just off Business Route 322 in Boalsburg. The chapel, which was part of the Columbus family castle in Spain, contains a cross of the type explorers planted on the shores of newly discovered territories. The Boal family brought the chapel to Boalsburg in 1909. You may visit daily except Tuesday, May through October. Guided tours are scheduled from 1:30 to 5:00 P.M. in spring and fall and 10:00 A.M. to 5:00 P.M. in summer. Write to the mansion at Boalsburg 16827, or call (814) 466-6210.

The people who live in Juniata and Mifflin Counties strive to uphold their heritage, their small-town way of life, and a standard of living not usually found in rural areas. Visiting here can be like a trip back in time, as you meet descendants of the early German settlers, including many Amish and Mennonite families. Any Wednesday during spring, summer, and fall, drop in on market day in Belleville (on Route 655, due west of Lewistown).

The stellar attraction in Mifflinburg is the **Buggy Museum** (523 Green Street), commemorating passenger carriages, not mosquitoes and bumblebees. The museum shows you where William A. Heiss manufactured horse-drawn vehicles from the late nineteenth to the early twentieth century, employing painters, blacksmiths, carpenters, and wheelwrights. Abruptly, the family shuttered the shop, and half a century passed before it was reopened, good as new. Visit the museum Thursday through Sunday, 1:00 to 5:00 P.M., May through mid-September; weekends only through October. For more information call (717) 966-1355.

Take a deep breath while driving to Northumberland, which has a big spot in history for such a little place. It was the home of Joseph Priestley, who is remembered for his pioneering work in chemistry, most notably the discovery of oxygen. His political thought influenced Thomas Jefferson in writing the U.S. Constitution, and he founded Unitarianism in America. Visit the scientist's laboratories at the *Joseph Priestley House* (472 Priestley Avenue), which is usually open Tuesday through Sunday from 9:00 A.M. to 5:00 P.M. and Sunday from noon to 5:00 P.M. It's closed Mondays and holidays except Memorial Day, July 4, and Labor Day. Call (717) 473–9474.

Most people driving along the Susquehanna River between Sunbury and Harrisburg take Routes 11 and 15 on the west side for speed; but on the east, the less-traveled Route 147 gives you lovely glimpses of the river valley and the interesting towns that dot the shores. In Millersburg, you can ride the *Millersburg Ferry,* one of the last surviving wooden, double-sternwheel paddleboats in the country. It runs a mile back and forth to Liverpool at one of the river's widest points. A Historic Landmark, the first ferry began operation in 1825, a big step forward for passengers and freight haulers using rowboats and pole boats. At the peak of river commerce, four boats made the trips. Now only the *Falcon* and *Roaring Bull* remain. A rough sign lettered on four boards nailed horizontally to a post says: FERRY IS RUNNING/DRIVE DOWN THE HILL/AND I'LL COME/AND GET YOU. You sort of have to guess when, knowing that the trip takes about twenty minutes each way. Each ferry accommodates four cars and fifty passengers. Without your car you could almost wade across, since the river at this point rarely goes more than 3 feet deep. To find the pickup point, drive into Millersburg on Route 147 and follow the signs. Generally, the ferry runs Memorial Day through September. Exact dates vary with the weather, the water, and the economy. For more information call (717) 692–2442, or write to the Millersburg Ferry Boat Association, P.O. Box 93, Millersburg 17061.

Across from the ferry landing, on the west side of the Susquehanna at *Liverpool*, lies *Hunters Valley Winery*. On a 150-year-old farm, the winery combines traditional wine-making methods with stainless-steel fermenters and fine filtration. Grapes come from vineyards that were planted in 1982. In many ways the growing conditions resemble those in parts of France, with full sun, good air circulation, excellent water drainage, and temperatures moderated by the river and mountains. You may walk through the vineyards and picnic on the grounds

Wednesday, Thursday, and Saturday 11:00 A.M. to 5:00 P.M.; Friday 11:00 A.M. to 7:00 P.M. Call (717) 444–7211.

Battlefield Territory

*D*on't miss *Gettysburg.* Yankee and Confederate soldiers fought the bloodiest battle of the Civil War here in 1863. The area is organized for tourism, with the absorbing history communicated in virtually every medium. *Gettysburg National Military Park* surrounds the city of Gettysburg. The visitors center (717–334–1124, extension 431) is across from the entrance on Route 134. Exhibits explain the battle, and battlefield tours start from here. The *Cyclorama Center* (717–334–1124, extension 422), complete with a sound-and-light show, centers around Paul Philippoteaux's 1884 painting, *Pickett's Charge.* Elsewhere in the center, displays of Civil War weapons and uniforms complete the picture. Because the battlefield is 6 miles by 7 miles, you may want to take a bus tour from the *Gettysburg Tour Center.* A stereo narration re-creates the Battle of Gettysburg during the two-hour tour. The center (717–334–6296) provides free shuttle service to and from major motels and campgrounds.

At least two dozen attractions related to the Battle of Gettysburg and the Civil War clamor for your attention, including the *National Civil War Wax Museum* (717–334–6245); the *Jennie Wade House*, home of Jennie Wade, the only civilian killed in the battle (717–334–4100); and the *Gettysburg Battle Theatre* (717–334–6100). *The Hall of Presidents* features

Hall of Presidents

wax reproductions of thirty-six presidents who relate American history in their own voices. For a complete listing of tourist territories, dining, camping, and lodging, write **Gettysburg Convention and Visitors Bureau**, 35 Carlisle Street, Gettysburg 17325, or call (717) 334–6274.

Also at Gettysburg, the **Eisenhower National Historic Site** commemorates Eisenhower's military and presidential years. The only way to get there is on a $5.25 tour that departs from the National Park Visitors Center. Your site visit includes the Eisenhowers' 230-acre farm and farmhouse, the only home the First Couple ever owned; a putting green and sandtrap given to the president by the Professional Golfers Association; a brick barbecue grill where he broiled 3-inch-thick steaks for guests; a skeet range; and the barn where Ike raised show cattle—but not the milk house where the Secret Service office was ensconced. The home first opened to the public in 1980, shortly after the president's widow, Mamie, died. Site manager Jim Roach describes the site as "a period piece" characterizing the fifties. "Eisenhower used this place for his style of personal diplomacy. On the porch he visited with Nikita Khrushchev in 1959, at the height of the Cold War, causing a slight thaw. De Gaulle, Churchill, and Adenauer visited this private place. Eisenhower invited them, he said, 'to get the measure of the man.' With all the trappings of office stripped away, world leaders came here and became real people." The trophies of Ike's life were not on display then, nor are they now. "If you visited when the Eisenhowers lived here—or now—you would never know that Eisenhower was the supreme commander of the Allied forces during World War II, let alone that he was president. The Eisenhowers were a couple who did not overwhelm you with their station in life." On the glassed-in porch stands an unfinished painting by Ike, who completed at least 260 others during the last twenty years of his life. The hours and the number of visitors allowed vary, so call first (717–338–9114).

Try to catch a live performance of James A. Getty as Abraham Lincoln. Since 1977 Getty and his wife, Joanne, have run **A. Lincoln's Place** (717–334–6049), a business centered around James' forty-minute

I Really Liked Ike

*W*hen I was ten, I made a pair of cufflinks for President Eisenhower. Enamel paint on metal, fired in a kiln at summer camp. Daddy drove to Gettysburg so that I could deliver

them personally. We handed them to a guard at a gate, then returned home. The president never sent a thank-you note, but I always assumed he wore my cufflinks.

Hog Maw—A Pennsylvania Recipe

*T*o make Hog Maw you need:

1 pig's stomach, well cleaned

2 pounds loose sausage

2 pounds diced potatoes

1 small diced onion

1 bunch parsley, chopped

Mix sausage, potatoes, onion, and parsley. Stuff mixture into stomach. Put on rack in roasting pan with enough water to cover the bottom of the pan. Cover. Roast 4 hours at 350 degrees. Remove lid and cook 15 minutes longer to brown. Serve with peas and applesauce or coleslaw.

performance as Lincoln. The show traces Lincoln's life from his boyhood in Kentucky through his presidency. The Gettys (no relation to the town of the similar name) came from Illinois, where James was a choral conductor, not an actor or historian. He grew a beard and, Joanne Getty says, "The beard made him do it." Getty immersed himself in research about Abraham Lincoln and began performing. The Lincoln impersonator tailors his shows to the age level of his audience. He performs at the **Conflict Theatre** (213 Steinwehr Avenue, Gettysburg; 717–334–8003) at 8:00 P.M. Monday through Friday in summer. Call to learn where you can see a performance by a man whose beard led him to study and portray President Lincoln.

To dine in the spirit of Gettysburg, drive 8 miles west on Route 116 to Fairfield and visit the **Historic Fairfield Inn**, in the plantation home of Squire William Miller, who laid out the town in 1801. In 1823 the building became an inn, and country cooking remains the big attraction. The inn also offers two guest rooms with shared bath. The restaurant closes occasionally for holidays and vacations, so reserve in advance. Write to P.O. Box 196, Fairfeld 17320, or call (717) 642–5410.

Drive to 900 High Street, Hanover, and take a deep breath. Fresh air? No. Fresh Utz (the name rhymes with *huts*, not *puts*) potato chips. Here is the factory of **Utz Quality Foods**, and you're welcome to take a free, self-guided tour Monday through Thursday, 8:00 A.M. to 4:00 P.M. Call (717) 637–6644 or (800) 367–7629.

Hickory Bridge Farm B&B in Ortanna offers nine rooms, including cottages, all with private bath. Two rooms have private whirlpools, too. Guest rooms are furnished with Pennsylvania Dutch antiques, and the cottages have wood-burning stoves. It's a genuine farmstead that boasts a red barn–turned–restaurant, a country museum with old farm equipment, a spring-fed swimming pond, and a trout stream, surrounded by fifty acres of farmland. In the restaurant you're offered amazing quantities of Pennsylvania Dutch cooking in a designer-country setting, Friday and Saturday nights and Sunday noon to 3:00 P.M. Call (717) 642–5261 for more information.

Southern Border

More Civil War history awaits at **Chambersburg**, which is west on Route 30. The Confederates occupied the city three times during the Civil War. The last time, in 1864, 3,000 Confederate soldiers rode into town demanding $100,000 ransom in gold. Chambersburg couldn't pay; the Confederates burned the town, putting two-thirds of its citizens out of their homes. Then the raiders rode off to McConnellsburg. Mention it the next time a Southerner complains about Sherman burning Atlanta. In the 1960s Chambersburg won recognition for efforts to preserve historic areas as part of city development plans. While the city could claim much history, actual historic buildings were in such short supply that saving them seemed especially important. Pick up a brochure with a mapped walking tour of downtown Chambersburg or a driving tour of the county at the Chamber of Commerce, 75 South Second Street, or call (717) 264–7101. Another useful resource is the **Cumberland Valley Visitors Station** at exit 6 off I–81 (1235 Lincoln Way East; 717–261–1200).

From McConnellsburg, take Route 522 north 30 miles to the **East Broad Top Railroad**, a National Historic Landmark at Orbisonia.

> **Trivia**
>
> On Route 30 between Chambersburg and Gettysburg, some air-brained chap has placed his mailbox on the side of the road, like everyone else's. Thirty feet higher, he has another one, marked AIR MAIL.

The Complete History of Shanty Beans

*E*denville is a town of 400 people, nestled up against North Mountain, near Chambersburg. There's one road in and one road out. A few times a year, the Edenville community center holds a fund-raising dinner, serving chicken, ham, and shanty beans. "About fifty years ago, three guys from Edenville were up on North Mountain hunting deer," says Allen Johnson. "It snowed, and they got stuck in a shack for four days. All they had to eat were lima beans, brown sugar, onions, and bacon. So Cham Clark, their cook, put all those ingredients together, and that's what they lived on. About twenty years ago, somebody got the bright idea to serve the beans—which they now call shanty beans—at the community center. Nope, they never got a deer."

East Broad Top Railroad

Some railroad buffs believe East Broad Top is the best train attraction in Pennsylvania. It is the last 3-foot-gauge (narrow-gauge) line in the East still operating from its original site. It was built in 1873 to move bituminous coal from the mines to Mt. Union, 11 miles north, where the "black diamonds" were dumped into standard-gauge Pennsylvania Railroad cars. The East Broad Top hauled coal until 1956. Today the 10-mile, hour-long, scenic, fun, and educational trip hauls railroad enthusiasts, excited kids, grinning grown-ups, photographers— and sound-recording zealots. People show up periodically, lugging audio equipment and stringing microphones along the track, to record the Doppler effect or to commit the train's distinctive chugs and choos to stereo for a film. You can stop for a picnic at the end of the line and come back on a later train. Trains leave 11:00 A.M., 1:00 P.M., and 3:00 P.M., weekends only, June through October. The fee is $9.00 per adult. Write East Broad Top Railroad, P.O. Box 158, Rockhill Furnace 17249, or call (814) 447–3011.

The town of Bedford, at the intersection of Route 30 and Business Route 220, developed in response to early influences of trading, transportation, and the military. A settlement was established in 1754; seventeen years later it was designated the seat of all lands west of Tuscarora Mountain. Today a 22-block National Historic District includes 210 structures considered significant from the Colonial period through 1930. Start at the visitors information center at 141 South Juliana Street. It's open Monday through Friday 9:00 A.M. to 5:00 P.M. and Saturday 10:00 A.M. to 2:00 P.M. For more information call (814) 623–1771 or (800) 765–3331. Pick up a map and information for a self-guided tour that includes fifty sites. One of these, the 1766 *Espy House*, was a private home when President George Washington chose Bedford as his headquarters. He was leading 13,000 federal troops to quell the rebellion of citizens in the "Whiskey Belt" against an excise tax on whiskey: the 1794 Whiskey Rebellion. This was the only time in American history that a president commanded the U.S. Army in the field. Bedford cheered President Washington as a conquering hero.

According to legend, Colonel and Mrs. David Espy planned a dinner party to honor the arrival of the president. A servant placed the main course, a wild turkey, on a windowsill to cool. A hungry solider, passing by on horseback, impaled the bird with his bayonet and rode off with it, thereby spoiling the president's dinner.

Elsewhere in Bedford you can see the trenches by the road where, in 1863, troops dug in against Confederate soldiers expected to attack the railroad at Altoona. The rebels marched toward Gettysburg instead, making the trenches unnecessary. President James Buchanan came to take the healing waters at the late, great Bedford Springs—a once-lavish resort begging to be renovated—where he kept his Summer White House. You can drive by, but that's it.

Pennsylvania's apple season runs from late summer through October, traditionally peaking the first of October. Thanks to advanced storage

Best Annual Events in South Central Pennsylvania

- Mid April, in Meyersdale, don't miss the Pennsylvania Maple Festival. From the Pennsylvania Turnpike, take exit 10 (Somerset), then Route 219 south. Write to the festival office at P.O. Box 222, Meyersdale 15552, or call (814) 634-0213.

- Memorial Day was born in Boalsburg in 1864 and declared a national holiday a few years later. The village celebrates annually with a *Day in Towne on Memorial Day*. From 9:00 A.M. to 5:00 P.M., it's crafts, food, music, and a reenactment of a Civil War event. At 6:00 P.M. everybody walks from the square to the cemetery, where cannon boom, a brass band and bagpipes play, scouts raise and lower the flag, and the VFW plays taps. If you're into Memorial Day, this is the Real Thing. Call (814) 466-6311 for more details.

- Nine free *Wednesday evening concerts-on-the-green* take place in June, July, and August in Johnstown. Call the Community Arts Center at (814) 255-6155.

- Early October is the *Railfest* at the Railroaders Memorial Museum, Altoona; (888) 425-8666.

- Third weekend of October, the *Fulton Fall Folk Festival* takes place in McConnellsburg. Heritage crafts and demonstrations, antique farm machinery, quilt show, apple-butter boiling, and more; (717) 485-4064.

techniques, the most popular varieties—Red Delicious, Golden Delicious, and Rome—are available nearly year-round. Call the Bedford County Visitors Bureau at (814) 623–1771 or (800) 765–3331 for a map of seven orchards that welcome your visit, plus bake shops, gift shops, and pizza shops to punctuate the tastes of Gala and Stayman apples. Adams County (717–334–6274) lists ten orchards.

Old Bedford Village re-creates a Pennsylvania community up to 1899, with more than forty log homes and craft shops, one-room schools, and other buildings brought from different places. While driving by on Route 220, you realize you're looking at a land before suburbs. Costumed guides and artisans demonstrate potting, making brooms, and weaving baskets. The activities sprawl over seventy-two acres, and a self-guided tour can take three hours if you explore all the options. Old Bedford Village is open daily except Wednesday; closed late October to mid-January. It schedules an almost continuous string of festivals and demonstrations. For further information write to 220 Sawblade Road, Bedford 15222, or call (814) 623–1156 or (800) 238–4347. Admission for adults is $7.00.

At the ***Jean Bonnet Tavern***, one of the oldest taverns in Western Pennsylvania (circa 1762), 4 miles west of Bedford on Route 30, the dining room and tavern are open daily beginning at 11:00 A.M. Call (814) 623–2250.

Seven miles west of Bedford on Route 30 is ***Coral Cavern***, the only known coral reef cavern, formed more than 300 million years ago while the area was covered by the Appalachian Sea. It's open for tours June and September weekends 10:00 A.M. to 5:00 P.M.; and daily July 4 through Labor Day. Halloween festivities are held in October on Friday and Saturday nights from dark until 10:00 P.M. Admission prices are moderate. Call (814) 623–6882 for details.

No cappuccino at the ***Coffee Pot***. No latte. Not even cream and sugar. Just a way-larger-than-life-sized coffee pot built in 1925, an example of the "programmatic architecture" that dotted the Lincoln Highway, Route 30, trying to lure tourists and travelers. The pot, located across the street from the Bedford County Fairgrounds, has been closed for years. You can't go in, but you can take silly pictures—or you can buy the whole pot.

Another dingbat installation on the Lincoln Highway is the **Ship Hotel**, a full-sized steamer marooned in the Allegheny Mountains, 17 miles west of Bedford. The ship, opened for intermountain crossings in 1932, is now closed and boarded. Pity. The sign outside still reads SEE 3 STATES, 7 COUNTIES. For more information on these unusual landmarks, call the Lincoln Highway Heritage Corridor (724–837–9750).

Consider a side-trip to Rainsburg, on Route 326, a community established so long ago that a nineteenth-century historian wrote, "the memory of man runneth not to the contrary," regarding its existence. The small borough features the **Rainsburg Male and Female Seminary**, incorporated in 1853 to offer secondary education and train teachers. And while you're in the area, stop in Chaneysville, a small town, also on Route 326, that sheltered fugitive slaves before the Civil War. For a wonderful look back in time, read David Bradley's excellent novel, *The Chaneysville Incident*.

In New Baltimore, milepost 129 on the Pennsylvania Turnpike, a church sits *on* the highway. Formally St. John the Baptist, a Catholic sanctuary, the church usually is called the **Church on the Turnpike**. Whether you're traveling eastbound or westbound, you can stop your car right at the church and walk to Mass. If you're driving you can take the Bedford or Somerset exit, both 20 miles away.

York

n 1903 William Harley decided to motorize his bicycle. He asked his friends, Arthur, Walter, and William Davidson, to help. Within four years, they had made 150 bikes. Visit the **Harley-Davidson Final Assembly Plant** (1425 Arsenal Road) in York, where more than 2,500 workers, many of them riders, make the cycles that let you feel the wind in your hair. Harley is the only major American-based motorcycle manufacturer. The tour includes a visit to the **Harley-Davidson Antique Motorcycle Museum**, where you can see military and police versions, dirt bikes and mopeds, and limited editions. "Old Harleys never die," legend says, "they go to museums." Hour-and-a-half tours are scheduled weekdays, but hours vary. Call toll-free (877) 746–7937 for details. Take I–83 and the Arsenal Road exit (9E) into York. Follow Arsenal Road (Route 30) 1 mile east.

Since York appeals more to country mice than to city mice, much of its allure is out of town. In Thomasville, for example, you can enjoy a free tour of the **Pfaltzgraff Factory**. (Even if you know the *p* is silent, it's not easy to say.) You need reservations for the tours, held weekdays by retired employees at 10:00 A.M. To watch stoneware, dinnerware, and accessories being manufactured, call (717) 792–3544 or write to Pfaltzgraff at Bowman Road, Thomasville 17364. You can also visit the company's Web site at www.pfaltzgraff.com. Today's production, mechanized and specialized, is a far cry from the simple methods the Pfaltzgraff family started using in 1811. But the finished dishes and bowls look the same. A few miles down Route 30, you can visit an outlet shop. To get there from York, drive 5 miles west on Route 30 and turn right on Bowman. You can't miss it because the factory's huge and you're driving 35 mph.

If you live or work at the *Shoe House*, tying those laces can be quite a climbing experience. The Shoe House, yet another quirky Route 30 delight, was built in 1948 by Mahlon Haines, who made shoes and boots for normal-sized folks. This butterscotch-colored building, originally a honeymoon cottage for Haines's customers, is 48 feet long and 25 feet high. For $3.00 (except in winter) you can tour the shoe, which is in Hellam, 3 miles east of York. For a bit less you can buy an ice cream cone. For more information, call the Lincoln Highway Heritage Corridor (724–837–9750).

PLACES TO STAY IN SOUTH CENTRAL PENNSYLVANIA

BEDFORD
Oralee's Golden Eagle Inn, 131 East Pitt Street; (814) 624–0800; oralee@bedford.net.

Bedford House Bed & Breakfast, 203 W. Pitt Street; (814) 623–7171 or (800) 258–9868.

DUBOIS
The Inn at Narrows Creek, 297 Treasure Lake; (814) 371–9394; fax (814) 375–7876; theinn@narrowscreek.com.

GETTYSBURG
Brafferton Inn, 44 York Street; (717) 337–3423.

JEANERSTOWN
Thee Olde Stagecoach Bed & Breakfast, 1760 Lincoln Highway; (814) 629–7440.

SCHELLSBURG
Covered Bridge Inn Bed & Breakfast, RR 2, Box 196; (814) 733–4093; www.bedfordcounty.net/cbi.htm.

STATE COLLEGE
Atherton Hotel, 125 South Atherton Street; (814) 231–2100.

SUNBURY
Danleys Hotel, 17 North Third Street; (717) 286–0127.

Edison Hotel, Market and South Fourth Streets; (717) 286–5605.

PLACES TO EAT IN SOUTH CENTRAL PENNSYLVANIA

DANVILLE
Old Hardware Restaurant,
336 Mill Street;
(717) 275–6615.

NEW BERLIN
Gabriel's Restaurant,
321 Market Street;
(717) 966–0321.

OSTERBURG
Slick's Ivy Stone Restaurant, Old Route 220;
(814) 276–3131. Open
April 1 through December
23; closed Wednesday.

SHAMOKIN DAM
Tedd's Landing,
Routes 11 and 15;
(717) 743–1591.

Southwestern Pennsylvania: Pittsburgh Region

Golden Triangle

Your visit to Southwestern Pennsylvania probably begins in Pittsburgh, a city that is right in the middle of the beaten path, a place where you can find unusual opportunities.

Pittsburgh is often called the Golden Triangle, in reference to its location at the confluence of the Allegheny, Ohio, and Monongahela Rivers. Why else would there be a Three Rivers Stadium? (Insiders call the Monongahela the *Mon.*) It can provide gilded experiences: The downtown bridges are painted gold, and the Steelers (football), Penguins (hockey), and Pirates (baseball) all have black-and-gold color schemes (colors that appear on the Pittsburgh city crest).

First, let's look back. From about 1870 to 1970, Pittsburgh led the nation in producing iron, steel, and glass and in mining bituminous coal. At the same time, Pittsburgh's environment rotted. Clouds rolled by on skies of black and gray, not blue, and nights sometimes glowed orange. Rivers flowed brown and green. Initial attempts at controlling smoke and floods were hampered by a few world wars and by a boom-and-bust economy. In 1941, the year Pittsburgh had the nation's highest rate of pneumonia, the mayor created a commission to eliminate smoke. Now, after decades of civic improvement, Pittsburgh has overcome its industry-induced pollution and renewed itself economically and environmentally. People who live here are proud of their

Trivia Tidbits

- *Pittsburgh-area high schools have produced five Hall of Fame–level NFL quarterbacks: Dan Marino, Joe Montana, Jim Kelly, John Unitas, and Joe Namath.*

- *The Three Sisters, Pittsburgh style, are not Eva, Zsa Zsa, Magda: They're the Sixth, Seventh, and Ninth Street bridges across the Allegheny River near downtown. Attribute their lyrical design to John Roebling, who also created the Aqueducts in Lackawaxen, Pennsylvania, and the Brooklyn Bridge.*

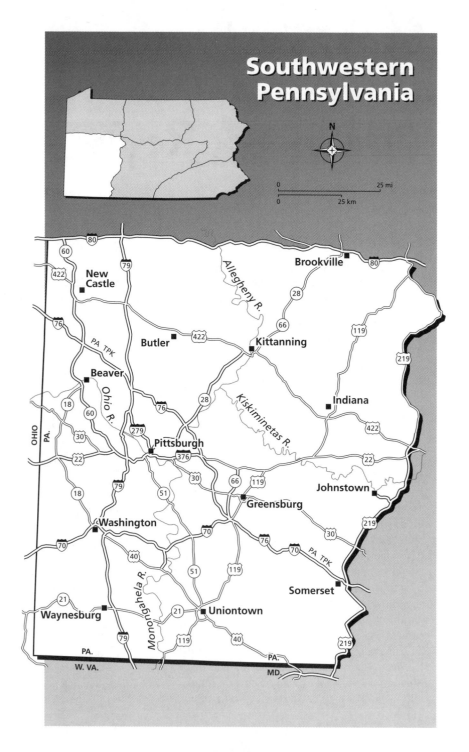

Southwestern Pennsylvania

SOUTHWESTERN PENNSYLVANIA

**AUTHOR'S TOP TEN FAVORITES IN SOUTH-
WESTERN PENNSYLVANIA**

Andy Warhol Museum

Banana split

*Beaver County World
Championship Snow
Shovel Riding Contest*

Fallingwater

Hyeholde's Restaurant

Jimmy Stewart Museum

Nationality Classrooms

Negro Mountain

Ohiopyle

Punxsutawney

hometown, calling it the Renaissance City. Pittsburgh today boasts a spectacular urban landscape, enjoyed by walkers, bikers, sportfishermen, and boaters. Let's stop talking and get moving!

The *Carnegie Museums* (4400 Forbes Avenue; 412–622–3131) were made possible by Pittsburgh's famous steel magnate and philanthropist, Andrew Carnegie. The *Carnegie Music Hall*, where most of Pittsburgh's major music organizations perform, seats 2,000 people. The *Carnegie Library* is considered one of the best public book collections in the country. The *Carnegie Museum of Art* features the work of nineteenth- and twentieth-century American artists, Impressionists and post-Impressionists. The philanthropist, who founded this museum in 1896, concentrated on "old masters of tomorrow"; today the collection focuses on fine arts, decorative arts, and architecture. The *Carnegie Museum of Natural History*, home of an impressive *Tyrannosaurus rex*, displays Egyptian artifacts, dinosaur skeletons (especially popular with kids), and interactive geology exhibits. Hours, admission fees, and special events vary.

The *Carnegie Science Center* (One Allegheny Avenue, next to Three Rivers Stadium), including the Buhl Planetarium, is full of hands-on exhibits. An "amusement park for the mind," it brings cryogenics and robotics to the level of interested parents and their kids—or kids and their parents. You can manipulate the foundation of a 30-foot water sculpture to play with hydraulics, follow a miniature railroad, and watch a four-story Omnimax movie. Sometimes you can get an overnight pass to explore till you drop—and beyond. Schedules for the attractions in the science center vary, as do admission rates. For full details visit www.csc.clpgh.org, or phone (412) 237–3400.

The *Pittsburgh Zoo* (One Hill Road; 412–665–3639) maintains more than 4,000 animals in habitats as diverse as an aquarium, an African savanna, and a reptile house. In the rain forest, endangered species such as gorillas live safely. The zoo is open daily 10:00 A.M. to 6:00 P.M., Memorial Day to Labor Day, and 9:00 A.M. to 5:00 P.M. the rest of the year. Closed Thanksgiving and Christmas. Moderate admission fee.

Circle the world in ninety minutes by visiting the University of Pittsburgh *Nationality Rooms* (157 Cathedral of Learning, 4200 Fifth Avenue). Twenty-four rooms, designed and donated by artists and architects from the city's ethnic groups, reflect the rich cultural mix of western Pennsylvania. Follow a time-and-place warp from fifth century–B.C. Greece, through first-century Israel, sixth-century Ireland, and on into the present day; see Baroque, Romanesque, and Byzantine styles without leaving Pittsburgh. Open year-round for tours, by appointment. (The *Cathedral*

Cathedral of Learning

of Learning, a forty-two–story Gothic stone tower, is itself a remarkable edifice.) A modest admission fee is charged. Phone (412) 624–6000.

Another unusual Pitt stop is the *Stephen Foster Memorial,* the world's only concert hall, museum, and library dedicated to an American composer. This native of Lawrenceville, Pennsylvania, the country's first professional songwriter, penned "Oh! Susanna" and "My Old Kentucky Home." Here you can see copies—and listen to recordings—of his 200 compositions and some musical instruments; you can also enjoy a broad cross-section of American pop culture from the 1850s to the 1930s. Regular hours are Monday to Friday, 9:00 A.M. to 4:00 P.M., and other times by appointment; $1.50 per adult. For information and reservations call (412) 624–4100, or write to University of Pittsburgh, Pittsburgh 15260.

For sidewalk browsing, try an area known as *The Strip,* between Smallman and Penn Avenues along the Allegheny River. This section, once entirely devoted to wholesale food markets, is still a great place to find fresh produce, fish, and cheese. Now that street artists and small shops have moved in, you can spend the morning browsing with a pastry in one hand and coffee in the other, investigating jewelry, pottery, and craft items.

Pittsburgh Trivia

- *The Pittsburgh International Airport is the first in the nation to start a fitness center for passengers and employees. With twenty cardiovascular machines and fifteen weight stations, it's calling your name. Forgetting your workout clothes is no excuse—you can rent an outfit, including shoes, for $3.00.*

- *Pittsburgh supplied most of the steel and cannons used by the Union Army during the Civil War.*

- *Pittsburgh has 70 miles of waterfront and more bridges than any other city in the United States. Worldwide, it ranks second in bridges to St. Petersburg, Russia.*

At 117 Sandusky Street, just across the Allegheny River from downtown, you'll find the *Andy Warhol Museum* (412–237–8300). It's not strictly off the beaten path, but the artist whose work it commemorates led such an idiosyncratic life and painted such avant-garde art, it belongs in this guide. Warhol, who raised Campbell Soup cans to a fine art, was born in Pittsburgh. Beginning in fourth grade, he took Saturday-morning art classes at the Carnegie Institute; at age seventeen he enrolled at Carnegie Institute of Technology, now Carnegie Mellon University. His famous images of Marilyn Monroe and Jacqueline Kennedy have changed the way Americans view portraits. Admission costs $6.00 for adults; during museum hours you can get into the great gift shop for free. Hours are 11:00 A.M. to 6:00 P.M.

Pittsburgh Firsts

- *Radio station, KDKA*
- *public television station, WQED, now home to Mister Rogers' neighborhood*
- *public library*
- *polio vaccine*
- *the Ferris wheel*

Wednesday and Sunday; it stays open two hours later on Thursday, Friday, and Saturday.

A few blocks away, in the historic Mexican War Streets section of the North Side, is the **Mattress Factory** (500 Sampsonia Way), a fascinating exhibit of contemporary and *nouvelle* art. The factory, which is, indeed, a converted factory, commissions, exhibits, and collects site-specific installations; it also provides living and working space for artists from around the world. Call (412) 231–3169, fax (412) 322–2231, or check out its Web site at www.mattress.org. Hours are Tuesday through Saturday 10:00 A.M. to 5:00 P.M., and Sunday 1:00 to 5:00 P.M. Admission costs $4.00 for adults, except Thursday, when it's free, and August, when it's closed.

Ohio River Valley

Immediately northeast of Pittsburgh, off Route 28, **Trillium Trail** delights wildflower enthusiasts, especially in early May. An easy half-mile walking trail reveals countless thousands of white trilliums blooming on the hillside above a ravine. This is first-rate for children, because the trail is not demanding. From Route 28 take the Fox Chapel Road exit and drive nearly a mile to Squaw Run Road. Turn left. A mile down the road you come to a fork; either choice leads to parking lots for the trail.

Nearby, **Audubon at Beechwood**, a property of the Western Pennsylvania Conservancy, has longer and more varied trails. Run by the Audubon Society, the reserve is great for wildflowers, birds, and photography. Eight marked, named footpaths range in length and ease of terrain, so some are perfect for young'uns and people new at observing nature, while others appeal to more rigorous tastes. Goldenrod Footpath, for instance, has a

They Came from Pittsburgh

Stephen Foster, composer; Billy Eckstein, musician; Sharon Stone, actress; Rachel Carson, conservationist; George S. Kaufman, playwright; Gene Kelly, actor and dancer; Willa Cather, author; Gertrude Stein, author; Shirley Jones, actress; Mary Cassatt, painter; Henri Mancini, composer; Perry Como, singer; and Jeff Goldblum, actor.

Trivia

The T is free. Between downtown stops, you can ride Pittsburgh's subway train, the T, for no charge.

gentle, easy slope; the Oak Forest path passes a deformed tree that shows how trees can respond to infections; and the Pine Hollow path smells best. The trails are open from sunup to sundown. Beechwood, formerly called Beechwood Farms Nature Reserve, includes a nature store and a Center for Native Plants, the region's only facility devoted solely to Western Pennsylvania's 1,500 native plants. Volunteers and staff provide maps, information, and advice on where to walk, depending on your stamina. Weekly guided nature walks are scheduled year-round. To get to the reserve, take Route 28. Take the Fox Chapel Road exit north and go nearly a mile. Turn left on Squaw Run Road, then right on Dorseyville Road. Beechwood Farms is almost 2 miles on the left. For more information write 614 Dorseyville Road, Pittsburgh 15238; phone (412) 963–6100.

You can appreciate history on a trip to **Old Economy Village** at Ambridge, less than an hour northwest of Pittsburgh. Old Economy is the preserved third and final home of the Old Harmony Society. In 1804 nearly 800 farmers and craftsmen, members of the Harmonists,

A Partial Listing of Movies Filmed in Pittsburgh

An Unremarkable Life	1989	Flashdance	1982
Angels in the Outfield	1951	Houseguest	1994
Bob Roberts	1991	Lorenzo's Oil	1991
Boys on the Side	1994	Milk Money	1993
Cemetery Club	1992	Money for Nothing	1993
Code Name Trixie	1973	Perils of Pauline	1914
Creepshow	1982	Rat Race	1960
Deer Hunter	1978	Revenge of the Living Zombies	1989
Desperate Measures	1996		
Devil and Sam Silverstein	1974	Roommates	1993
Diaboloque	1995	Silence of the Lambs	1990
Dominick and Eugene	1988	Simple Justice	1988
Drive-In Madness	1987	Slapshot	1977
Fish that Saved Pittsburgh	1979	Waterland	1991

Trivia Tidbits

- *What were they thinking when they filmed these two movies in Pittsburgh?* Bloodsucking Pharaohs of Pittsburgh *and* Poland: Two Weeks in Winter?

- *The Nickelodeon, the earliest form of public film exhibition, opened on Smithfield Street in Pittsburgh in 1905.*

- *The Pittsburgh Pirates are the second-oldest professional athletic team in the country. Originally called the Alleghenies, they changed their name when other teams accused them of "pirating" players from their rosters.*

migrated to America from southwest Germany seeking religious and economic freedom. They spent ten years in Butler County, Pennsylvania, and ten years in Indiana before returning to the Keystone State to stay. Each time, at each locale, they named their community Harmony. The Harmonists based their simple, orthodox lifestyle on beliefs of the early Christian Church. Because they expected the second coming of Christ to happen at any moment, they adopted celibacy to purify themselves for Christ's thousand-year reign on earth. Religion came first in their lives—they celebrated the Last Supper six times a year—but their communal lifestyle was not austere. Harmonites ate well, adorned their furniture, played music, planted flower gardens, and made money for the community. The society developed economically and technologically; by 1825 they built cotton and wool factories powered and heated by steam engines, a steam laundry, and a dairy. They constructed shops for blacksmiths, hatters, wagonmakers, and linen weavers. Their canny business sense produced fine furniture, sturdy buildings, beautiful grounds, and many beneficial investments in the nearby towns. The community lasted until 1905.

Your hour-long tour takes in the community kitchen, the cabinet and blacksmith shops, granary, wine cellar, tailor shop, store, great house, and gardens. Tour guides know much about both the religious beliefs and the history of the community. When an old object has been moved or when restoration somehow deviates from the original structure, the guides point it out and explain. The village and its gift shop are open Tuesday through Saturday, 9:00 A.M. to 4:00 P.M., and Sunday noon to 4:00 P.M. The last tour begins at 3:00 P.M. The village is closed Mondays and holidays, except Memorial Day, July 4, and Labor Day. Moderate rates are charged. For information about daily tours and special events, write Harmonie Associates, Fourteenth and Church Streets, Ambridge 15003, or call (724) 266–4500. To get there, follow I–79 exit at Coraopolis south, and take Route 65 along the Ohio River to Ambridge.

Just across the Ohio River, but still in Pennsylvania, is a rural estate that's fun to visit with the kids. At ***Hidden Hollow Farms*** in Aliquippa, you can see cows and horses, wildlife and gardens, all summer long. Hike, picnic, and photograph the day away. Even the mailing address is adorable: 103 Hidden Hollow Lane, Raccoon Township, Aliquippa 15001. Call (724) 378–9966 for more information.

A poke and a plum away (poke your head out the car window and you're plum outta town) is Beaver, on Route 68 between Routes 51 and 60. Here you can visit the **Richmond Little Red School**, a one-room schoolhouse used from 1844 until 1950, now restored with many original furnishings. A group of local volunteers, some of whom received the first eight years of their education in the red-brick school, joined forces to revive it. They host and guide visitors, answering questions about what it was like to study 'rithmetic there. The original bell hangs over the door, the pump out front has been painted red to match the brick, and the outhouse (not identical to the original but a genuine outhouse, nonetheless) does what outhouses have always done. Because the building gets cold in winter and the potbellied stove heats slowly, the volunteers prefer not to schedule tours in winter. The school is open Sunday, 2:00 to 5:00 P.M., in June, July, and August and other times by appointment. Write Park Road, Beaver 15009. You can call (724) 775–3452; if you're lucky, someone will answer.

Four miles and a few minutes north of Rochester, still on Route 68, New Brighton offers the **Lapic Winery**, operated by Paul and Josephine Lapic. It's open daily for wine tasting and sales, except on election days and major holidays. Call ahead (724–846–2031) to arrange tours, surf to www.mlapic@usaor.net, or write 902 Tulip Drive, New Brighton 15066.

Romance Is Alive and Well and Living in Pennsylvania

*O*n the day after Thanksgiving, Phil Schild takes Jean to Hyeholde's Restaurant in Coraopolis, near the Pittsburgh airport. After Phil's filet and Jean's rabbit, Phil kneels and proposes. Jean, of course, accepts—who wouldn't?—and they proceed, over cheesecake, to make wedding plans. Six weeks later, on January 7, they marry in Philadelphia during the Blizzard of '96. Only half the sixty invited guests are able, willing, or crazy enough to venture out into 30 inches of snow. The marriage and the romance survive, as Phil and Jean traverse the Pennsylvania Turnpike almost monthly to visit family. Wouldn't it be nice if the Turnpike offered frequent-driver programs? Whenever possible, they dine at Hyeholde's.

Westsylvania

Slightly farther north you'll find **McConnells Mill State Park**, which appeals to historians, geologists, rock climbers, birders, botanists, hunters and fishermen, rafters, and, of course, picnickers. The park gets its name from a restored gristmill, which you can reach by parking in a lot near the top of the hill and following a footpath down. You may take a free guided tour of the mill in the summer or visit on your own. Through the park runs Slippery Rock Creek and its adjacent walking trail. Be sure to venture toward **Slippery Rock Gorge**, 20,000 years old and 400 feet deep. For details about tours, hunting, and fishing, phone (724) 368–8091. Take I–79 to the Route 422 exit. Go almost 2 miles west on Route 422. A sign indicates a left turn for the park.

The town of Slippery Rock—home of the former Slippery Rock State Teachers College, now **Slippery Rock State University**—resembles most college towns, with music stores and coffee shops. One resident said the recent addition of a McDonald's made the place "big time." Then came Burger King. If the town's name sounds familiar, it's because many football stadiums in the country announce the Slippery Rock scores at the end of their games. Enough people have been titillated by the name to generate some funny stories about its origin. According to the best yarn, one day the Big Chief of the Native Americans was standing by the creek and slipped on a rock. "This is a slippery rock," he said.

Between Erie and Pittsburgh, I–79 is largely rural, scenic, and lightly traveled. Roughly halfway between these cities, it's worth taking some

My Heroine

She beats the guys, she beats the rugged teens, she beats absolutely everybody. She's my heroine, Sharon Silkroski, and she's a champ. For five consecutive years, from 1993 through 1997, Silkroski won the Beaver County World Championship Snow Shovel Riding Contest. Then, like any true champ, she announced her retirement when she was at the top of her game. But the 1998 race was canceled for lack of snow, and in '99 her crazed fans lured her out of retirement. She won again. Silkroski, who was a postal clerk when she started racing, is now a case manager in a retirement center. A resident of Baden (rhymes with made in), she averages eleven seconds for the 160-foot-long shovel-racecourse. She rides a neighbor's shovel, which spends the rest of the season on display in a garage. How does she do it? Luck? Talent? Training? "I can't tell you," whispers the winner. "If I tell you, I'll have to kill you." Surely there are worse ways to beat the winter blahs.

time to go both east and west on Route 208. Near the intersection of I–79 and I–80, the easterly road goes into Grove City, where signs direct you to *Wendell August Forge* (620 Madison Avenue). The forge is a self-contained industry in the middle of a quiet community, one of the few remaining forges in the country that still fabricates aluminum, pewter, bronze, and sterling silver pieces by hand, without any production machinery. Wendell August determined that he could forge, or hammer, light metals rather than cast them, so he opened the forge in 1923. Originally the forge produced ornamental gates, grills, and tables for large, institutional buildings. At the end of each job, August presented the customer with a small bowl or vase from the forge. These gifts turned out to be so popular that he began producing gift items for sale.

Today the forge is operated by the Knecht family, who bought it in 1978. Die cutters create the designs, and thirty-five master craftspeople hand-hammer the items over a fire and hand-finish them. No two pieces are alike. You can walk through part of the forge to see the entire process in action and ask the craftspeople questions. All items produced at the forge are for sale in the showroom for prices ranging from a few dollars to a few thousand. Free plant tours for individuals are available Monday through Saturday, 9:00 A.M. to 4:00 P.M.; the showroom is open Monday through Thursday and Saturday, 9:00 A.M. to 6:00 P.M.; Friday until 8:00 P.M.; and Sunday, 11:00 A.M. to 5:00 P.M. Call (724) 458–8360 or (800) 923–4438.

Going west on Route 208 from I–79 takes you to Volant, about 10 miles from Grove City, and, 4 miles farther, to New Wilmington, the historic home of Westminster College. This is the heart of a refreshingly noncommercial Amish area.

Golf, anyone? You might think that Atlanta and Palm Springs have the best golf courses. And, indeed, they might. But the nation's *first* golf course, or at least the oldest course in continuous use, is near where you are at this very moment: in Foxburg. One Joseph Mickle Fox learned the game of golf from a pro at St. Andrews, Scotland. He returned to his estate in Foxburg with golf clubs and balls made of gutta-percha, a tough, rubbery substance made from the latex of Malaysian trees. In 1887 Fox built a five-hole course for the enjoyment of his neighbors, with greens of sand and one-quart tomato cans serving as cups. To erase footprints from the sand, the golfers used long poles with burlap bags nailed to the end. Fox paid a man $15 a year to use a scythe to keep the fairways clear and playable. Three holes were added, then one more, bringing the modern total to nine. Since its inception the course has seen continuous play and is now the *Foxburg Country Club*. Midweek fees are $10 for nine holes, $16 for eighteen holes (which means playing the nine holes twice); weekends and holidays, prices go up. Fore!

The club houses the **American Golf Hall of Fame** and the P.G.A. Hall of Fame library and museum. The nostalgic log structure contains a museum chronicling 400 years of golf. The museum, golf course, and club house are open daily, April through October. For more information and for tee times, call (724) 659–3196. The Foxburg Country Club is located just minutes south of exit 6 of I–80 on Route 58 in Foxburg.

Three miles from Foxburg, the wild and scenic Allegheny River runs through a spectacular and densely forested valley, where quaint Victorian homes lie just across the river in Emlenton (near I–80 exits 5 and 6). At the corner of Main Street and Second stands America's first steam-powered grist mill. Built in 1875, the refurbished **Old Emlenton Mill** serves as a central point for an annual Christmas in Oil Country celebration.

Southwest Corner

Southwest of Pittsburgh, where the state borders West Virginia, Pennsylvania presents many winning, off-the-beaten-path discoveries. At the intersection of I–70 and I–79 is the town of Washington, where you can visit the **LeMoyne House Historical Museum** (49 East Maiden Street), Pennsylvania's first National Historic Landmark of the Underground Railroad. In the house, built in 1812, you can learn about life before the Civil War. A nineteenth-century apothecary exhibit fills one room, and exhibits on local history change regularly. You might find a display on Victorians at home, for example, or nineteenth-century wedding gowns. Another interesting feature, way off the path most people want to follow, is the crematory LeMoyne built, the first in the Western Hemisphere; you can tour it on Saturday only, May through September, 2:00 to 4:00 P.M.

Just outside, the garden contains medicinal herbs that Dr. LeMoyne used in his medical practice, plus culinary herbs and fragrant and flowering herbs for pleasure. Volunteers tend the garden, changing plants and shrubs frequently. You can take a self-guided tour of the garden and see, in addition to mint, foxglove, and brown-eyed Susans, a Native American grinding stone and milemarkers from the old National Highway. And, lest you think old-timers were out of touch, look at the upping stone—a safe way for travelers to step off the stage coach. Wouldn't you love one to access and exit your sport-utility vehicle? Tours run February through mid-December, Tuesday through Friday, 11:00 A.M. to 4:00 P.M., and weekends, noon to 4:00 P.M. Admission costs $4.00 per adult. Call (724) 225–6740 for last-minute details. While you're at LeMoyne House, peek at the guns and uniforms in the **Southwest Pennsylvania Military Museum**, a repository of memorabilia from all of America's wars. The book and gift shop offers an array of history-inspired products. Appropriately, the Washington County Historical Society also operates from the LeMoyne House.

Also in Washington, tour **Bradford House** (175 South Main Street), once the home of David Bradford, a leader in the Whiskey Rebellion of 1794. The home is furnished in antiques of the period and is open May 1 to December 20, Wednesday through Saturday, 11:00 A.M. to 4:00 P.M.; Sunday 1:00 to 4:00 P.M. Candlelight tours are held one weekend in December. The admission fees are modest; here, too, there's a gift and book shop. Call (724) 222–3604.

A great place to take children is **Meadowcroft Museum of Rural Life**, about 20 miles northwest of Washington. (Go north on Route 844, then west on Route 50.) People have lived and worked on the land at Meadowcroft for 14,000 years—longer than at any other documented site in North America. Here you can see how Native Americans, frontier settlers, farmers, lumbermen, and coal miners shaped the history of western Pennsylvania. Step back in time and spin wool from the museum's flock of sheep, or watch a blacksmith forge red-hot iron. There are also a gift shop and cafe, outdoor picnic tables, and long, lovely wooded paths. Meadowcroft Village is open Memorial Day through Labor Day, Wednesday through Saturday, noon to 5:00 P.M.; Sunday 1:00 to 6:00 P.M. Call (724) 587–3412, or write ahead to 401 Meadowcroft Road, Avella 15312.

Trivia
The Underground Railroad, the system used to help free Southern slaves, traversed Pennsylvania. See historic markers in Sugar Run, Rummerfield, Towanda, Ulster, and elsewhere.

If you're interested in unique towns for their own sake, travel southwest from Washington on Route 40, almost to the West Virginia border, to Good Intent, at the headwaters of Wheeling Creek's Robinson Fork. Nobody knows how the village got its name. In the early 1800s Peter Wolf built a gristmill here, but the mill pond filled up with silt, so he had to start over downstream. The town never got around to creating a main street. Two gristmills, two blacksmiths' shops, a tannery, a stage company, a harness and saddle shop, a post office, and a Baptist church have come and gone. Nobody teaches in the schoolhouse; somebody lives in it. The general store sells only stoves and is open only on Saturday. The town doesn't have a local government, but it has an unofficial mayor, who lives elsewhere. Folks who live here like it the way it is. They say that among the things Good Intent doesn't have are crime, hurry, legal contracts, and selfishness. People help one another in times of sickness. They seal agreements with a handshake. Maybe that's what Good Intent means.

Three miles east of Waynesburg (take exit 3 off I-79) the **Greene County Historical Museum**, a mid-Victorian mansion, features period antiques; a country store; and collections of pottery, glass, quilts, and Indian and early-American artifacts—over 10,000 items in all. The site once housed the county poor farm. Little is known about the operation of the poor farm except that after an extremely unfavorable review of the home by the *Atlantic Monthly* in 1886, a reform campaign was launched to improve the conditions. The museum is open May through October, Wednesday to Sunday, for a modest fee. Hours vary, so call (412) 627-3204 for information.

If museum antiques make you lust for some oldies of your own, you might visit **June Stout Antiques**. Stout's antiques fill her Federal-style, 1858 brick home plus seven other buildings, just outside the village of Ruff Creek. She sells only one-of-a-kind, handmade pieces at least a hundred years old—books, vintage clothes, china, and dining tables large enough to seat fifty. She'll show it all to you, entertaining you with a running commentary on the antiques, the neighbors, her family, and anything else that comes to mind. "My son says to take a nerve pill when you come in," she jokes. "I'm a little crazy. Anything I buy is for sale." Gifts, though, you can't buy at any price—"but I don't get many gifts." Call ahead (412-627-6885) to make an appointment when she's in town. Take I-79 to exit 4 at Ruff Creek, then go 1/2 mile north on Route 221.

Jimmy Stewart Meets the Groundhog

R emember the movie *Groundhog Day*, in which Bill Murray plays a grumpy TV weatherman who has a really bad day—over and over and over again? Murray tries to learn from his mistakes—and turn the page on the calendar. Check out the scene for yourself in Punxsutawney.

In Punxsutawney (rhymes with *chunks a saw me*), Punxsutawney Phil, the groundhog, officially does or does not see his shadow at dawn on February 2, determining whether we will or will not have six more weeks of winter. The televised event takes place on Gobbler's Knob, a mythical, magical area, before an audience of media and more than

35,000 people. The town sits where Route 119 crosses Route 36. For more information call (814) 938–7700 or (800) 752–7445.

The groundhog tradition stems from beliefs associated with Candlemas Day and the days of early Christians in Europe. According to an old English song:

> *If Candlemas be fair and bright, Come,*
> *Winter, have another flight;*
>
> *If Candlemas brings clouds and rain, Go,*
> *Winter, and come not again.*

As the home of the renowned weather prognosticator, Punxsutawney, a captivating turn-of-the-twentieth-century town, assumes pomp and circumstance near the second of February. Many of Punxsutawney's nostalgic Main Street building facades have been renovated, and beautiful tree-lined West Mahoning Street features Millionaires' Row, preserved from the days when Punxsutawney was a thriving coal, oil, and lumber town.

In the children's library of the Mahoning East Civic Center, downtown Punxsutawney, a window lets kids watch Punxsutawney Phil between his on-duty days. Who knows what Phil will predict next year? The shadow knows.

Even if groundhogs are the animals with the biggest reputation in metropolitan Punxsutawney, they're *not* the biggest animals. Bison are. At **Nature's Comeback Bison Ranch**, the Hineman family raises bison. The large mammals may end up on your table (as food, not in a failed broadjump attempt, one hopes), but they're happy, well-fed, free-range bison in their lifetimes. "Many people are amazed at how playful bison actually are," says owner Brian Hineman. "They have been seen throwing logs that weigh over 500 pounds several feet in the air and bouncing around like little lambs. Bison can run up to 45 miles an hour—amazingly fast

My Grandchild, the Groundhog

*I*n our house, Groundhog Day has special significance. Our oldest son, Dan, earned a doctorate studying the behavior of marmots, which are groundhogs that live at altitude. Since neither Dan nor our other sons has produced offspring, we consider groundhogs our grandchildren. Bizarre? When you're old enough to be a grandmom but no one lets you be one, stuffed platypuses look cuddly. Why not groundhogs?

for their massive size." The breeder bull bison, who weighs over a ton, is called Bossman. The ranch, which has been in the family for over 150 years, was initiating field tours as this book went to press, so you should call ahead (814–427–2544) to reserve a place as off the beaten path as imaginable. (Watch where you step as you get up close and personal with these large animals.) To produce healthier meat with lower fat content, Nature's Comeback feeds them only hay and grass. The meat, says Hineman, "tastes like your best cuts of beef without the waste of trimming the fat." You can write to Nature's Comeback Bison Ranch, RD 2 Box 174, Punxsutawney 15767 or reach it at hineman@key-net.net. Take I–80, exit 16, 1 mile off Route 119 south.

Trivia

In 1868, in the Jacks (Oak Hall) School in Porter Township, Clarion County became the home of the Anti-Horse Thief Association. Although there is no record of a horse's being stolen for several decades, the Association holds an annual dinner. In 1976, when Dwight D. Eisenhower and Arthur Godfrey belonged, it cost $1.00 to become a life member.

A trip to nearby Smicksburg is an enjoyable drive, particularly at harvest time. Home of the largest Amish settlement in western Pennsylvania, Smicksburg has a lovely rolling landscape freckled with farms. Motorized vehicles share the winding roads with horses and buggies, and you find fine craftsmanship and craft shops at every turn. Because of the strong religious faith, many shops close on Sunday.

On Route 219, 4 miles north of Grampian, you can find **Bilger's Rocks**, a phenomenon of massive, ancient sandstone formations, called "rock city," covering some twenty acres. One 500-ton boulder rests on a smaller one in perfect balance. Visited for centuries, these giant sandstone formations tower 30 to 50 feet. Call (814) 236–3508 to learn about tours, usually held May through October.

From groundhogs to bison to rabbits. Or at least invisible rabbits. Okay, *one* invisible rabbit. You know, Harvey, the bunny only Jimmy Stewart could see in the movie *Harvey*. Jimmy Stewart's life and films are alive and well and entertaining everyone at the **Jimmy Stewart Museum** in Indiana, Pennsylvania. Sit back in a 1930s-style movie theater and watch *Mr. Smith Goes to Washington* and *It's a Wonderful Life*. The small museum occupies the third floor of the public library, and it's dedicated to the homeboy who catapulted from his family's hardware store to the heart of Tinseltown. Admission should cost $5.00 per adult, and the museum should be open from 10:00 A.M. to 5:00 P.M., Monday through Saturday, and noon to 5:00 P.M. Sunday and holidays—but the place is about as calm and laid-back as Jimmy himself, so call ahead to check. The library is at Ninth and Philadelphia Streets, and the mailing address is Box One, Indiana 15701. Call (724) 349–6112 or (800) 83–JIMMY (that's really 800–835–4669).

Noah weathered a flood, but he heeded the warning. The town of Johnstown did not. Late in May 1889, it started raining. The neglected South Fork Dam, upriver of Johnstown, gave way May 31, and a wall of water moved 14 miles downstream, plucking chairs, doors, walls, and complete houses out of their rightful places. The water immersed and erased the industrialized city in ten minutes, killing more than 2,200 people. The *Johnstown Flood Museum* (304 Washington Street) recreates this shocking episode—the catastrophe of death and homelessness, followed by the triumph of human spirit that allowed the town to rebuild. Every hour the museum shows *The Johnstown Flood*, which won the 1989 Academy Award for best documentary short subject. One survivor expresses the drama: "My boyhood home was crushed like an eggshell before my eyes, and I saw it disappear." See the flood in 3–D, in books, and in souvenirs at the museum. Write to P.O. Box 1889, Johnstown 15907–1889. (Same ZIP code as the year of the flood.) Call (814) 859–1889 or (888) 222–1889, float through the Web at www. ctc-net.net/jaha. Adults pay $4.00 to get in. Hours are daily, year-round, 10:00 A.M. to 5:00 P.M.; from May through October, it stays open two hours later on Friday and Saturday.

Two years after the flood, the Cambria Iron Company (a predecessor of Bethlehem Steel Corporation) began building houses in the community of Westmont, 500 feet up Yoder Hill from downtown Johnstown. Since no roads existed, the company assembled a vertical commuter system, which remains today as the *Inclined Plane*, which rises at a grade of seventy-one percent. The *Guinness Book of Records* ranked it the steepest vehicular inclined plane in the world. Originally designed to carry people and their horses and wagons, it now accommodates people and their cars. In 1935 Bethlehem Steel sold the railway for a dollar to Westmont Borough, which leases it to the Cambria County Tourist Council for $10 a year. The wheels, rails, and other parts came from standard railway equipment (and, in fact, the cars are duplicates of those that hauled cargo boats over the Allegheny Portage railroad). The Inclined Plane is composed of two sets of tracks implanted in the side of the hill; two cars run simultaneously, one going up and the other going down. The cables, three on each side, are 2 inches in diameter and 1,130 feet long. They can safely carry 337,000 pounds, or 167 tons. Here's the fun part: You may ride it. You can access the top from Route 56 or Route 403 and the bottom from Route 271. Above the funicular hangs an American flag that measures 30 feet by 60 feet. For more information call

(814) 536–1816, or write 711 Edgehill Drive, Johnstown 15905. Hours from Memorial Day weekend to Labor Day are Monday to Thursday, 6:30 A.M. to 10:00 P.M.; Friday and Saturday, 7:30 A.M. to midnight; and Sunday, 9:00 A.M. to 10:00 P.M. The rest of the year, it's open 6:30 A.M. to 10:00 P.M., closing only on January 1 and December 25. Round-trip fare for an adult pedestrian is $3.00. Add more for the kids and the Edsel. Adults over 65, with ID, ride free during nonpeak hours.

At the top of the Inclined Plane is Westmont, originally called Tiptop. Take time to explore this appealing Victorian enclave, a bit of small-town America where you wish you grew up. Locals say the town has always been divided in two parts: the more affluent southern section with single-family homes, called the "dinner" side, and the less affluent northern section with twin homes and smaller singles, called the "supper" section. Westmont attracts naturalists, too: Lucerne Street contains the longest municipally owned stand of American elm trees east of the Mississippi (even small towns like a claim to fame). Although half of all American elms were killed by Dutch elm disease, this beautiful, stately "cathedral arch" of elms is maintained. The borough now has nine trees that qualify as historic elms, which means they measure at least 10 feet in circumference at chest height.

If you have a pioneer spirit, follow Route 219 south to Somerset and visit the **Somerset Historical Center**, which portrays rural life in southwestern Pennsylvania from the rugged pioneer struggles of the eighteenth century through the commercial agrarian enterprises of the mid-twentieth. You can see utensils, machinery, and restored buildings. Guided tours are supposed to take place year-round, from 9:00 A.M. to 5:00 P.M. Tuesday through Saturday and from noon to 5:00 P.M. on Sunday. Hours vary, however, so call ahead at (814) 445–6077. The center closes all holidays and all Mondays, except Memorial Day, July 4, and Labor Day. Write to the historical center at R.D. 2, Box 238, Somerset 15501.

Laurel Highlands

*E*veryone who visits—or lives in—Pennsylvania should see *Fallingwater*, the summer retreat that architect Frank Lloyd Wright designed for the Pittsburgh department-store owner Edgar J. Kaufmann. The house, completed in 1939, was constructed of sandstone quarried on the property and was built by local craftsmen. It's the only remaining Wright house where the original setting, furnishings, and artwork remain intact. Fallingwater reflects Wright's genius, which allows the house to merge with its environment outside and to echo outdoor nature in its stone and wood interior. The house, appearing to grow out of the boulders and rocks, extends over a natural waterfall of Bear Run. You can't see or hear the water from inside, but you can do both from any balcony or from a stairwell down from the living room. A gray sandstone four-story chimney at the core of the house anchors it into the stone cliff. Wright built a desk in every bedroom and placed all headboards on eastern walls so that no one would be awakened by the sun. No wonder he was a genius! The home retains a feeling of seclusion and oneness with the natural environment, even though many people visit. The house is open for tours from mid-March through November, daily except Monday, 10:00 A.M. to 4:00 P.M. In December and March it is open only weekends, and it's closed January and February. Phone ahead for reservations, especially during July, August, and October, the busiest months. Try to get there during midweek, and plan to wear comfortable walking shoes. For more information write P.O. Box R, Mill

Fallingwater

Run 15464 (724–329–8501). Fallingwater is about two hours southeast of Pittsburgh via the Turnpike, on Route 381 between the villages of Mill Run and Ohiopyle (pronounce it *Ohio pile)*.

Fallingwater—the house that could be called *A River Runs through It*—is maintained by the Western Pennsylvania Conservancy. At the end of your tour, guides invite you to watch a short film about the organization's activities. The film is fascinating, and the work of the conservancy lifts your spirits. You may decide to join, even if you live out of state. Children under age nine may not tour Fallingwater, but for $2.00 an hour they can stay in an on-site childcare center. Forty-five–minute tours cost $8.00 midweek and $12.00 on weekends and holidays; they are scheduled from 10:00 A.M. to 4:00 P.M. For an in-depth two-hour tour, scheduled each morning at 8:30, the cost is $30 midweek and $35 on weekends.

You may have heard that Fallingwater is falling, and indeed it is. A steel I-beam now supports the famous cantilevered dwelling, and engineers, architects, and historians are deeply engaged in finding affordable solutions to repairing the structure while continuing to accept tourists. You must call for reservations anyway; just be prepared for disappointment.

West of Ohiopyle, 7 miles along a scenic mountain road, you can find another remarkable installation of Wright's craft: **Kentuck Knob**, a smaller, simpler home that Wright designed for the Hagan family of Uniontown. A dramatic yet serene place, the house is hexagonal, with hexagonal accents, all native fieldstone and tidewater red cypress. It hides in—rather than sitting on—the mountain it occupies, so you're practically at the front door before you see it. The home has an open

Fifteen Grandkids and One Covered Bridge

*K*enneth Pletcher grew up in the rural farming community of Sculton, near Connellsville. He was a high school graduate, which was cool, but his parents were shopkeepers, which was not. Kenneth was in love with Amanda, daughter of a farming family, who was expected to go to college and return to run the farm. When Kenneth proposed, Amanda's dad said no. So on the day she graduated from high school, Kenneth picked her up from the steps of the county courthouse, and they motorcycled to Elkton, Maryland, where they married. "Fifteen grandchildren later," says their grandson, Jon Pletcher, "they're still happy, still going strong. And we still have family reunions in Sculton and always visit their private covered bridge."

floor plan—with a heating system under the floor—with giant expanses of glass to enjoy the panorama of the Youghiogheny (rhymes with *sock a say knee*) River Gorge and surrounding mountains. The name? Probably, says site manager Susan Waggoner, someone was heading for Kentucky and stopped here. A knob is a low, rounded hill. On the grounds behind the visitors center is an oversized apple core by artist Claes Oldenburg. The house, opened to the public in 1996, is open for tours most of the year between 10:00 A.M. and 4:00 P.M., daily except Monday. 'Swonderful. In December through March, call for hours. It costs $10 per adult midweek, $15 on weekends. Write for reservations (suggested) at Kentuck Knob, Box 305, Kentuck Road, Chalk Hill 15421; or call (724) 329–1901.

Now's a perfect time to stop for a walk or a picnic along the Youghiogheny River at **Ohiopyle State Park**, almost 18,500 acres of wilderness delight. The Youghiogheny Gorge, cut 1,700 feet into the Laurel Ridge by the river, takes your breath away. Totally contained within the state park is the borough of Ohiopyle, almost two whole blocks long. Sixty-five people live here, and commercial establishments include a grocery store with a small cafe, a gas station, and, in season, a Dairy Queen and a pizza parlor. Oh, yes, and four whitewater river outfitters. "The name of the town, Ohiopyle, is subject to fact and fiction depending on who you're talking to," says Mayor Mark McCarty. The state park's interpretation is something like "white frothing water," but if you study the early settlers' writings, it's more "like peaceful river." The water in this case is the Yough (rhymes with *sock*), Youghiogheny being an Indian word for "flowing in a roundabout course." Yes, it's off the beaten path, says Jim Greenbaum, manager of White Water Adventures. "On the other hand, there are two interstate highways within a half hour of here." Ohiopyle has lured tourists since the early 1900s, when people came by train from Pittsburgh and Washington to swim in the river and hike on Fern Cliff. Once three large hotels dominated the borough. Then "the railroads went away," as Greenbaum puts it. In the early 1960s, a new industry—whitewater rafting—was born. The season for rafting runs March through October, with the bulk of tours scheduled from mid-May until mid-September.

The Middle Yough, says Greenbaum, is the easy section, great for kids over five or first-time adults. The Lower Yough is intermediate, recommended for people age twelve and older. The Yough sections called Pure Screaming Hell, Bastard, and Double Pencil Sharpener are recommended for rafters with the most technical expertise—but then, so is Cheeseburger Falls. If you'd like to try a rafting trip, call one of the four outfitters with state concessions:

White Water Adventurers, P.O. Box 31, Ohiopyle 15470. Phone (724) 329–8850 or (724) 329–5986 or (800) 992–7238; fax (724) 329–1488; Web site: www.wwaraft.com.

Laurel Highlands River Tours, P.O. Box 107, Ohiopyle 15470. Phone (724) 329–8531 or (800) 472–3846, fax: (724) 329–8532; e–mail 4raftin@laurelhighlands.com.

Mountain Streams & Trails Outfitters, P.O. Box 106, Ohiopyle 15470. Phone (724) 329–8810, (800) 723–8669, or (800) 245–4090; fax (724) 329–4730; Web site: www.mtstreams.com.

Wilderness Voyageurs, P.O. Box 97, Ohiopyle 15470. Phone (724) 329–1000 or (800) 272–4141; fax (724) 329–0809; e–mail rafting@wilderness-voyageurs.com; Web site: www.wilderness-voyageurs.com.

The latest innovation at Ohiopyle is the immensely popular *Youghiogheny Bicycle Trail,* part of the national rails-to-trails movement. This section is part of the connection between Pittsburgh and Washington, D.C., following the right-of-way of the abandoned Western Maryland Railroad. Seventeen miles of the *Allegheny Highlands Trail* have been completed, traveling through the communities of Garrett, Rockwood, and Markleton. "No one ever dreamed people would drive to ride a bicycle trail," says Greenbaum. "But they do. And the wonderful thing is, the Yough trail follows the river, and it's flat." Since the trail is level, it's accessible to bicyclists and hikers of all abilities.

This trail has changed two things. First, people who can't or are afraid to raft or who have babies can hike or ride the bike trail, keeping up conversations with their friends on the water. A bicycle actually goes faster than a raft, so it's an easy ride. Second, people can ride their bikes and gauge whether they can handle the river. Some people who have avoided rafting ride their bikes along the trail and decide they can handle it. Plus, every party might want to name a designated biker to schlep and safeguard the picnic lunch and video camera. You can rent bikes at *Country Trail,* 7 Bridge Street, Rockwood 15557 (814–926–2117); *Mountain Sports,* 750 North Center Avenue, Somerset 15501 (814–445–2115); or *Wilderness Voyageurs,* Commercial Street, Ohiopyle 15470 (800–272–4141). Check out the latest on the trail at www.atatrail.org, or visit www.dcnr. state.pa.us/stateparks/parks/ohio.htm for park info.

If the luxury of a Frank Lloyd Wright home makes you pine for an upscale night or two, consider *Nemacolin Woodlands Resort and Spa* in Farmington. With French food, French paintings, and a par-72 golf course, its motto could be "extravagance R us." Elegantly appointed guest rooms include marble baths, private voice mail, and plush terry-cloth robes. Entertainment for kids, a shopping mall, and a climbing wall are on the premises. The place is named for a Delaware Indian named Nemacolin who, in 1740, carved a trail through the Laurel Mountains between what is now Cumberland, Maryland, and Brownsville, Pennsylvania. When congress established the National Highway in the mid-1800s, the highway incorporated Nemacolin's trail. For resort reservations, log onto www.nwlr.com, or call (724) 329–8555 or (800) 422–2736.

Route 669 leads you straight to (well, not really straight, but toward) *Mt. Davis* in the *Forbes State Forest*—at 3,213 feet above sea level, the highest elevation in the state. (So it's not the Rockies—wanna make something of it?) An interesting speck of geological lore is the scattering of small, concentric stone rings caused by localized frost heaves. Each ring surrounds a spot in the soil that is a bit softer and looser than the adjacent ground. When the ground freezes, the soft spots rise and become minibumps. Surface rocks on these bumps, or humps, slide off; as this process repeats itself over thousands of years, the sliding rocks deposit themselves in ring-like formations. Cool! Not far away is the aptly named *High Point Lake.* Hiking trails and picnic sites abound. For more information write to the Bureau of Conservation and Natural Resources, Bureau of Forestry, Box 519, Laughlintown 15655, or call (724) 238–9533.

Mt. Davis is actually a rock that sits atop *Negro Mountain.* A ten-page brochure about the area doesn't mention the origin of the name until page nine. "For 150 years after the first colonies were established," says the brochure, "Negro Mountain was untouched by white man." Presumably it was also untouched by white women and African-American people of both sexes. The brochure says that the Indians claimed the land. In the mid-1700s British and French settlers developed a political and economic interest in the area. Various versions of the story agree that "a large, powerful black man valiantly distinguished himself in a battle with the Indians." He died—and was hastily buried in an unmarked grave—on the mountain, which was thus named for him, or at least for his race. Originally the mountain was a thousand feet higher, say geologists, and it is one of the area's oldest rock formations. Weather is an important factor; frost has been observed during every month of the year, which clearly is not true for the surrounding areas. Wildfires have severely damaged portions of Negro Mountain. Marked hiking trails cover the area.

If you're into gallows humor, pop up Route 281, nearly to I–70, and go to the courthouse in Somerset. The building served as the county jail from 1856 to 1981, and the double hanging gallows is still intact. Who hanged together? Twins? Tea for two? Now the building holds county offices. What do you think they do to employees who are habitually late?

In Hopwood, just before Uniontown, is an unusual emporium called the *Art Warehouse* (Route 40 at Bennington Road), an eclectic gallery where you can find the original work of more than 150 artists and artisans. Necklaces, vases, statues, and furniture cover 5,000 square feet in this warehouse of an art store. For hours call (412) 439–1667, fax (412) 439–1048, or write Box 69, Hopwood 15445.

If you love art, glass, and what's now called art-glass, you'll enjoy the *Youghiogheny Station Glass and Gallery* (900 West Crawford Avenue, Connellsville), located in (surprise) the renovated, restored, and resplendent Youghiogheny train station in Connellsville. Amid the seasoned ticket office, departure board, and lighting fixtures, you can explore a collection of Tiffany-style lamps and other decorative items, all for sale. The station, built in 1911, rates a spot on the National Register of Historic Places, and the collection rates a four-star listing on the must-see register of crafters' sojourns. The back room sells 120 colors of stained-glass sheets from the Youghiogheny Glass company. Hours are Thursday, 10:00 A.M. to 7:00 P.M.; Sunday, noon to 4:00 P.M.; and all other days, 10:00 A.M. to 5:00 P.M. Call (724) 628–0332 for more details or to learn about stained-glass classes. All aboard!

Best Annual Events in Southwestern Pennsylvania

- *Beaver County World Championship Snow Shovel Riding Contest,* held in Economy Park on the third Saturday in January, unless there's too little snow. Call (724) 782–0212 or (800) 342–8192.

- In Punxsutawney, *Groundhog Day* is held February 2. Watch television news, and you'll be there.

- On the first Sunday in May, the *Giant Eagle/City of Pittsburgh Marathon* attracts runners from near and far. Call (412) 281–7711 or (800) 359–0758 for details.

- In mid-May the *National Road Festival* celebrates the historic national road, US Route 40. Food, fun, and entertainment stretch for 90 miles along the National Road Heritage Park. Call (724) 329–1560 for details.

- At the end of May, Johnstown marks the anniversary of the 1889 flood at the *Johnstown Flood Museum.* Call (814) 539–1889 or (888) 222–1889.

- The Oakland Church of God (in Distant, just south of New Bethlehem) salutes America and its veterans by creating a

Living Flag Extravaganza. Annually, sometime around Memorial Day or July 4, the church choir take their places among the stripes and stars and sing an evening's worth of patriotic songs. Oh, say, can you see a reenactment of the flag-raising at Iwo Jima? Admission is free, but offerings are appreciated. For this year's dates, call the church at (814) 275-3626.

- Punxsutawney holds its *Groundhog Festival* the last full week in June. The festival, an annual do since 1966, features band concerts, street dances, fireworks, and a chili cook-off. Call (814) 938-7700 or (800) 752-PHIL.

- In early August, enjoy barbecue and bluegrass at the Frank Lloyd Wright–designed home, *Kentuck Knob,* in Chalk Hill. Get more info at (724) 329-1901.

- *Antique Flea Market,* Somerset, second Saturday in August. Call (814) 445-6431.

- For four days in August, the *Three Rivers Regatta* takes over Pittsburgh's waterfronts. Call (412) 281-7711 or (800) 359-0758 for details.

- In August the *Western Pennsylvania Wild Flower Festival* blooms in Rimersburg. Contact the Southern Clarion County Development Corporation, P.O. Box 705, Rimersburg 16248.

- During the second weekend in August, show your heritage at the *Sligo Irish Festival.* Call (814) 745-2074 or (814) 473-8149 to learn what the shamrock is planning this year.

- Saddle up yer bronco, or at least your sport-utility vehicle, and head to the *North Washington Rodeo,* on Route 38, 16 miles north of Butler, during the third week in August. Daily performances at 8:00 P.M. feature men doing saddle bronc, bareback, and calf-roping and women running barrel races. There's always something at intermission for the kids and raffles for the grown-ups. You might win a registered colt or a steer that the rodeo organizers have purchased from the local 4-H group. For more information call (724) 637-3266.

- *Knox Horsethief Days,* third week in August. Knox is located near exit 7 of I-80. If you fancy sidewalk sales, parades, and chicken barbecues, be there. For more information write to the Knox Borough Office, Knox 16232.

- During the second weekend in September there's a flax scutching festival at Monticue's Grove in Stahlstown. If the town's not off the beaten path enough for you, the event surely is. Here you can see how craftspeople used to take the flax plant and dry it, process it, and weave it—scutch it, in other words—until it became linen. To learn more about scutching or the festival at the second-oldest flax scutching festival in the world, call (724) 238-9244.

- New Bethlehem initiated its annual *Peanut Butter Festival* in 1996 to promote the Smucker's peanut butter plant. If you think toast and jelly are naked without p.b., visit Gumtown Memorial Park on Water Street on a weekend in mid-September. Call the nutty people at the New Bethlehem Chamber of Commerce (814-275- 3929) for details.

- The third weekend in September, Washington County holds a *Covered Bridge Festival.* Call (800) 531-1414 for details and which eight of the twenty-three "kissing bridges" hold what events.

- The *Pennsylvania State Fishing Tournament* takes place the last week in September in Tideoute (rhymes with pretty suit). Call (800) 624-7802.

- Head to the *Ohio Rowing Regatta* in Pittsburgh each October. Call (412) 281-7711 or (800) 359-0758 for details.

- Just before Christmas, the Oakland Church of God, which brings you the living flag, presents a *Living Tree.* The "tree," alive with the sixty angelic voices of the choir, towers more than 20 feet in the air. Admission is free, but offerings are appreciated. For this year's dates, call the church in Distant at (814) 275-3626.

- December 31, celebrate *First Night* (it's really Last Night, isn't it?) throughout downtown Pittsburgh. Call (800-744-3378) for details.

PLACES TO STAY IN SOUTHWESTERN PENNSYLVANIA

BEAVER FALLS
Beaver Valley Motel, Route 18; (724) 843-0630 or (800) 400-8312.

DAYTON
Rebecca House Bed & Breakfast, Church and Rebecca Streets; (814) 257-8232.

FARMINGTON
Stone House Bed-and-Breakfast, 3023 National Pike; (724) 329-8876.

HARRISVILLE
As Thyme Goes By, 214 North Main Street, Box 493; (724) 735-4003.

INDUSTRY
Willows Inn, Route 68; (724) 643-4500.

NEW BETHLEHEM
Rod & Rifle Bed & Breakfast, 234 Broad Street; (814) 275-4410.

PITTSBURGH
Sunnyledge Boutique Hotel, 5124 Fifth Avenue; (412) 683-5014.

The Priory, A City Inn, 614 Pressley Street; (412) 231-3338.

PUNXSUTAWNEY
Jackson Run Bed and Breakfast, Mill Street Extension, off Route 36; (814) 938-2315.

Pantall Hotel, 135 East Mahoning Street; (814) 938-6600.

SLIPPERY ROCK
Applebutter Inn, 666 Centreville Pike; (724) 794-1844.

SOMERSET
Bayberry Inn, 611 North Center Avenue, Route 601; (814) 445-8471.

VOLANT
Candleford Inn Bed and Breakfast, Box 212, Mercer Street; (724) 533-4497.

WAYNESBURG
Cole's Log Cabin Bed and Breakfast, Pine Bank; (724) 451-8521.

Greene Gables Bed and Breakfast, 1015 East High Street; (724) 627-4391.

PLACES TO EAT IN SOUTHWESTERN PENNSYLVANIA

ACME
Brady's, Route 31; (724) 423-4566. Or surf for your dinner at www.bradys@westol.com.

BEAVER FALLS
Giuseppe's Italian Restaurant, Route 18; (724) 843-5656.

BRIDGEWATER
Dockers Restaurant and Tavern, 500 Market Street; (724) 774-7071.

BROOKVILLE
The Meeting Place, 209 Main Street; (814) 849-2557.

Pittsburgh loves wedding soup, an Italian dish: chicken broth, tiny pastina noodles, spinach, and sausage meat balls. Divine.

CORAOPOLIS
Hyeholde's Restaurant, 190 Hyeholde Drive; (412) 264–3116.

FARMINGTON
Stone House, 3023 National Road; (724) 329–8876. Casual fine dining.

PITTSBURGH
Underground Café, in the Andy Warhol Museum, 117 Sandusky Street; (412) 237–8300. Open Wednesday to Sunday, 11 A.M. to 6 P.M.

SCENERY HILL
Century Inn, Route 40; (724) 945–6600. Casual dress in building from 1724.

SLIPPERY ROCK
Wolf Creek School Cafe, 664 Centreville Pike; (724) 794–1899. Located in a restored one-room schoolhouse.

WAYNESBURG
AJ's Landing, 1140 East Roy Furman Highway; (724) 852–2571.

Rohanna's Restaurant and Lounge, R.R. 2; (724) 627–3778.

Willow Inn, R.D. #4, Oak Forest Road; (724) 627–9151; www.willowinn.com.

Northwestern Pennsylvania: National Forest

The Lake District

The tourist literature says the Erie area is "Erie-sistible." And why not? It has a great lake—make that a Great Lake—a Native American history 300 years long, and a location way off the beaten path. Ohio, Lake Erie, and New York state form the western, northern, and eastern borders of Erie County, and getting to Erie from anywhere in Pennsylvania means driving through miles and miles and miles of woodland and uninhabited terrain.

A few decades ago, Lake Erie was pronounced dead. But it wasn't really dead; the problem was actually too much of the wrong kinds of life. Nutrients such as phosphates and nitrates, especially plentiful in agricultural runoff, encouraged excessive growth of algae, which grew so fast that they choked out other forms of plants and fish. The process is called eutrophication. In water where no oxygen can reach the bottom, the only fish that can live are small pan fish. As Lake Erie deteriorated, only pan fish survived. A massive combined effort by area manufacturing companies, local colleges, state and federal governments, and concerned citizens turned things around. The City of Erie improved its sewage disposal system. Now the Department of Health tests regularly for harmful bacteria. Industries treat their wastes so that they won't hurt the lake. Colleges run ecology projects, continuously monitoring the state of the water. At least one Erie councilman pilots his boat, at cost, for the monitoring teams. Game fish have returned. In fact, the city celebrated when the first coho salmon was caught after the long, empty spell.

Part of the success story comes from the central role that Lake Erie plays in the lives of the people who live here. Hundreds of people go to the public dock in the city every day, if not to fish, at least to check out conditions. Adults who've lived here all their lives talk about

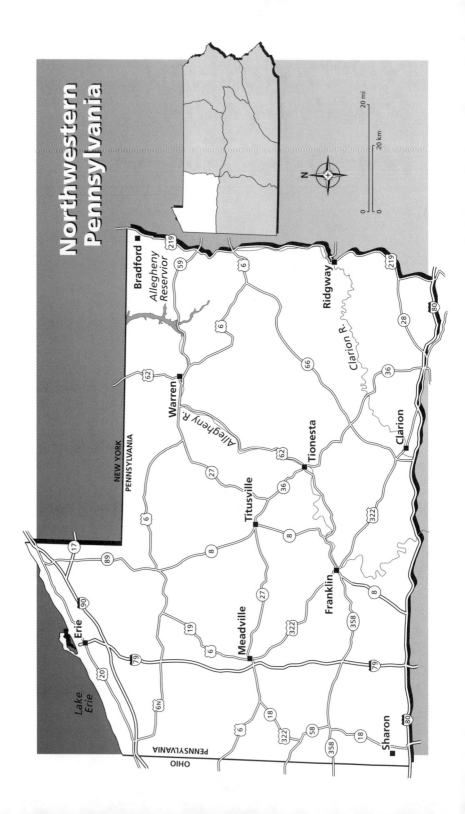

Northwestern Pennsylvania

having gone out fishing every morning before school or every evening after school. This spirit affects what it feels like to visit the lakeshores. The passion is contagious. Among the most ardent fishers are many members, including the past prioress, of the community of Erie Benedictine Sisters, whose main house is on East Lake Road. The sisters get out in boats of varying reliability to relax with nets and poles. They've developed expertise in cooking the fish that don't get away; one recipe involves baking coho salmon in a mixture of mushrooms, French dressing, and Parmesan cheese. The sisters certainly talk about their vocations and ministries, about religious life, about helping the needy, and so on—but they're also wonderful folks to consult about fishing.

The best place to learn about Erie and the lake is **Presque Isle State Park** (rhymes with *press tile*). One of the most remarkable places in Pennsylvania, it offers enough outdoor recreation to keep you busy for weeks. It's a 3,200-acre peninsula extending from the City of Erie (just 4 miles west of downtown) into Lake Erie. Although in French Presque Isle means "almost an island," this area has been a real island several times. Storm waves have broken through the neck of land, isolating the distant portion at least four times since 1819. One gap remained open for thirty-two years. Interestingly, the combined effects of erosion on one side and sand deposits on the other change the peninsula's shape and location noticeably, not in thousands of years, but in just a few. Geologists call it a recurving sand spit and estimate that the peninsula has moved about 1/2 mile east in the past hundred years. Of course, that doesn't make it any harder to find. The Stull Interpretive Center, located at the beginning of the park near Barracks Beach, displays maps showing the changes. If you avoid the peak summer swimming season, it's possible to walk for hours along the beaches and in the woods without seeing another human being.

The diverse nature of Presque Isle is astounding. It has six distinct ecological zones, each with a unique plant and animal community. Due to the peninsula's location along the Atlantic flyway (that's the celestial interstate system for migratory birds), more than 320 species of birds have been recorded here. They usually visit in April, while heading north, and again in November, because Presque Isle offers one of the best avian bed-and-breakfast systems around. At the tip of the peninsula, Gull Point is designated a restricted, protected, fragile ecosystem—a place you may not enter between April 1 and November 30. You may, however, bring binoculars to nearby spots and look up, up, and away. The interpretive center offers sophisticated displays and literature on migration and on species of flora and fauna as well as child-geared material on butterflies and ducks.

Speaking of children . . . they probably want to head for the beaches, where the surf is usually high enough to be interesting without getting rough enough (in good weather) to be dangerous. Follow the rules: Swim only when and where posted. Do not dive, even from the shoulders of a friend. Don't climb on dunes. Keep your pets on leashes no longer than 6 feet. Do not feed wildlife, including park rangers. Near Grave Yard Pond you can rent rowboats, canoes, and motorboats, but stay tuned to Channel 16 for boating conditions. The park is open from dawn to dusk. Presque Isle State Park has almost as many phone numbers as species of

Lighthouse at Presque Isle State Park

gulls: For details about the Stull Interpretive Center, sports concessions, guided nature tours, movies, and lectures, phone (814) 833–0351. To reach the marina in season, call (814) 833–0176. To reach the lifeguard office in season, call (814) 833–0526 You can also surf to www.dcnr.state. pa.us or write to the park at Box 8510, Erie 16505.

For boating on a grander scale, visit the restored *U.S. Brig* **Niagara** in Erie. The ship, captained by Oliver Hazard Perry during the War of 1812, commemorates the victory on September 10, 1813, when nine American ships triumphed over the British fleet on Lake Erie—the first time in naval history that a British squadron was defeated and captured. The *Niagara* and Perry gave the world the famous line: "We have met the enemy, and they are ours." (See the *Niagara* on special Pennsylvania license tags. They're tan and brown, and from a distance they look as faded as a pair of sixties bell bottoms.) Visiting the *Niagara* used to be a landlubber's proposition; but now that the restoration is complete, the ship has been commissioned and is back in the water in sailing condition. The restoration process was almost as dramatic as the events that made the square-rigged, two-masted ship important in the first place. Her reconstruction called for skills not widely found in the United States—to season and shape the pine and fir, to make the sails, and to forge the custom metal parts used in the rigging. The program involved teaching historical maritime crafts to young men and women of the Pennsylvania Conservation Corps. The *Niagara* is administered by the Pennsylvania Historical and Museum Commission.

The *Niagara,* berthed at the foot of Holland Street, is the official flagship of Pennsylvania and is the tallest tall ship on the Great Lakes, which she often tours. In order to schedule *your* hour-long tour, you need to know whether she's in port while you're in Erie. Tours usually

Four Erie Lighthouses (814–452–3937)

- **Presque Isle,** *residence of park superintendent. Exterior viewing daily 8:00 A.M. to sunset.*

- **North Pier,** *located at the south entrance of the channel. Viewing daily.*

- **Lighthouse Street,** *first built 1818,*

replaced in 1856; no light since Christmas Eve 1899. Exterior viewing daily.

- **Perry Monument,** *located at Misery Bay; dedicated to those who died in the 1913 Battle of Lake Erie in the War of 1812.*

take place April through October, Tuesday through Saturday, 9:00 A.M. to 5:00 P.M.; and Sunday, noon to 5:00 P.M. Phone (814) 452–2744, sail to www.brigniagara.org, or write to 150 East Front Street, Erie 16507. Moderate admission fees.

If you still have your sea legs, you can ride the thirty-six–passenger water taxi that starts at Dobbins Landing and stops at the Water Works and the marina entrance. Weather permitting, the taxi operates daily from 10:00 A.M. to 6:00 P.M. You can take a forty-five–minute sight-seeing harbor tour on the *Little Toot* daily from 10:30 A.M. to 9:00 P.M. Call (814) 454–5892. Or, last but still wet, take a two-hour or day-and-a-half cruise on the 85-foot schooner *Appledore*. For rates, schedules, and information call (814) 459–8339.

Another action-oriented display is the ***Firefighters Historical Museum*** (428 Chestnut Street), which is in the old #4 Erie Firehouse. It contains more than 1,300 items of fire department memorabilia, including old uniforms and equipment and an 1830 hand pump. The museum is open May through August, 10:00 A.M. to 5:00 P.M. on Saturday and 1:00 to 5:00 P.M. on Sunday. From September through October the museum is open from 1:00 to 5:00 P.M. Saturday and Sunday. Call (814) 456–5969 for details.

The ***Erie Historical Museum and Planetarium*** (356 West Sixth Street), housed in a twenty-four–room mansion from the late 1800s, has exhibits on regional and maritime history, including the Battle of Lake Erie. Other rooms contain decorative arts and period rooms with outstanding woodwork and stained glass. The planetarium, in the carriage house, re-creates the movements of the sun, planets, and stars. The museum is open Tuesday through Sunday, 1:00 to 5:00 P.M.; the planetarium showings are Saturday at 2:00 P.M., Sunday at 2:00 and 3:00 P.M., and Tuesday through Friday at 2:00 P.M. Additional hours are scheduled for the museum and planetarium in the summer; call (814) 871–5790 for details.

Kids in Erie love the ***ExpERIEnce Children's Museum*** (420 French Street, 2 blocks from the waterfront), where they can paint their faces, dance on a stage, and learn what owls eat for dinner. Kids under two enter free, and others pay $3.50. The museum is open Wednesday through Saturday, 10:00 A.M. to 4:00 P.M. and Sunday, 1:00 to 4:00 P.M. In July and August it's also open Tuesday. Call (814) 453–3743, fax (814) 459–9735, or e-mail junep@vpo.net. The Web address is ecm-erie.org.

In the same complex, called Discovery Square, are two other museums. The ***Erie History Center*** (419 State Street) focuses on county history. Phone the center at (814) 454–1813; fax (814) 452–1744; or e-mail echs@velocity.net. The *Erie Art Museum* (411 State Street) has a small permanent collection and changing exhibits of fine art. Phone (814) 459–5477, or e-mail erieartm@erie.net.

To see contemporary American jewelry, studio pottery, carvings, and textiles, stop at the *Glass Growers* (701 Holland Street, 814–453–3758). Upstairs are the creations of local and regional artists. The shop is open Monday through Saturday, 10:00 A.M. to 5:00 P.M. Their offerings have proved sufficiently popular to warrant opening a satellite store at Village West, a shopping center with a New England–style setting on Twenty-sixth Street. To get there, take the West Twenty-sixth Street exit off I–79. Call the main store for more details.

You've been through town, yet you haven't heard a word about the barges filled with lumber, coal, and hay. Where, oh where, is the *Erie Canal*, you wonder. It started on the Elk Creek, a scant 20 miles down Route 5 from the city of Erie, and carried barges to the Hudson River, thus linking the Great Lakes and the Atlantic Ocean. The canal opened in 1844 and began to lose business to the railroads as early as the 1850s. When the aqueduct over Elk Creek collapsed in 1872, the canal closed. At least it survives in song. Beginning in 1918, commercial traffic began using the larger New York State Barge Canal.

> **Trivia**
>
> *Strange but true. The only statue of George Washington wearing a British uniform is on High Street, next to the historic Eagle Hotel (now a restaurant and museum) in Waterford. Call (814) 796–6990 to reach the restaurant.*

Elk Creek flows through the town of Girard, which has a unique place in American history: Dan Rice lived there. Dan *who*? Dan Rice, the circus owner whose carnival spent summers in Girard. Dan Rice, whose flag-waving clown costume included a top hat and balloon pants. Dan Rice, whom Thomas Nast, an artist from *Harper's Weekly*, caricatured—and whose image became known as "Uncle Sam." *That* Dan Rice.

Wine Country

From Erie, continue east on Route 5 to visit the local wine region, which stretches about 100 miles along the coast yet extends only 5 miles inland. Wine grapes flourish here because the lake creates a microclimate in which cold spring winds blow in from the lake, keeping the plants from budding too early and being vulnerable to frost. In the summer, lake breezes cool the vineyards and keep the air circulating; in the fall the stored summer warmth from the lake delays frost. Because the lake once was much larger and has receded, the soils along the shore are especially fertile. Hence, fine wine. (Let's drink to that.)

In North East stop at the **Hornby School Museum** (10000 Colt Station Road, Route 430) to visit the restored one-room schoolhouse in the style of the 1870s. With a reservation, you can arrange to experience the kind of lessons that would have been part of a typical school day. The school is open Sunday from May through October, 1:00 to 5:00 P.M., and by appointment. Call (814) 725–5680 for more information.

Trivia

So many fish are being fed at the Linesville Spillway, on Route 6 west of Meadville, that ducks can walk on the fishes' backs to compete for bread.

More fun than school, perhaps, **Lake Shore Railway Museum** (Wall and Robinson Streets) also has a lot to teach. Two children cried all the way there one morning because they hate museums, but at 5:00 P.M. attendants had to chase the kids out of the train cars to close up. The museum displays historical railroad items from the nineteenth and twentieth centuries, ranging from dining-car china to signaling devices. Outside the museum, which is in a station house by the tracks, you may tour a caboose and railroad cars on the siding—a Pullman sleeping car, diner, freight car, coach, and baggage car. The wooden caboose looks like the olden days, complete with a stove and cooking area. In front of the station is a fireless steam locomotive, built in Erie in 1937. The schedule of the museum varies with the season and includes some special holiday events, so call ahead (814–825–2724) for specific details.

Oil Country

et Meadville lure you off the Interstate (off I–79, to be precise). **Allegheny College**, one of the oldest colleges west of the Alleghenies, has a good collection of Abraham Lincoln memorabilia in the Pelletier Library. Ida Tarbell, one of the college's first female students, majored in biology because she hoped to find God with what she could learn through a microscope. After graduating, she became one of the muckrakers famous at the turn of the twentieth century, journalists who tried to expose the abuses of businesses and the corruption of politics. Miss Tarbell wrote an extensive biography of the Lincolns and later donated the papers to her alma mater. The library also has many interesting papers, books, and artifacts related to Miss Tarbell. Two college buildings, Bentley Hall and Ruter Hall, are listed on the National Register of Historic Places.

Meadville's downtown includes more than a dozen historic buildings that should interest those who care about old architecture. You can pick up a free self-guided tour to bygone Meadville at Market House (910 Market Street). The Crawford County Tourist Association office is on the second floor. On the ground floor a farmers' market flourishes, as it has for more than a hundred years. You can eat at the lunch counter and shop through the produce, flowers, baked goods, handicrafts, cheese, ceramics, and collectibles in the marketplace. Market House is open year-round.

Approximately 30 miles east of Meadville, you can get a fascinating glimpse of the early influence of oil, before Texans thought of liquid gold. Start at Titusville with the **Drake Well Park and Museum** (814–827–2797) site of the world's first successful oil well. The well is topped by a replica of the derrick. The museum details the early oil days and shows a twenty-five–minute film about how the first well came to be drilled. In the library are thousands of photographs plus papers of Ida Tarbell related to her famous exposé of the Standard Oil Company. (Tarbell's family had been involved in the beginnings of the oil industry, a background that drove her to write about oil.) Her scrapbooks,

Drake Well Park and Museum

including clippings of some of her reviews, present the story at a personal level, quite different from the accounts in history books. Oil apparently has been generating press and publications for as long as drilling has unearthed it, because the museum boasts 3,500 books, 1,000 periodicals, and 1,000 newspapers dealing with early oil news. There's also a collection of 4,000 glass-plate negatives from the work of John A. Mather, an early photographer of oil scenes. The park is 1/2 mile southeast of Titusville on Route 8. The museum is open from 9:00 A.M. to 5:00 P.M. every day, except November 1 to the end of April, when it is closed all day Monday and until noon Sunday. Closed on major holidays year-round.

A short drive southeast on Route 27, then south on Route 227, brings you to Plumer. Go 1 1/2 miles farther south to the ghost town of Pithole, which was an oil boomtown in the late 1860s and was abandoned

Best Annual Events in Northwestern Pennsylvania

- In late July, *Discover Presque Isle Days,* run by the Presque Isle Partnership. Call (814) 838–5138.

- A stilt-walking Uncle Sam leads the parade at the annual *Dan Rice Days* in Girard. Held the first Saturday in August, the festival includes games, food, crafts, and such—and Uncle Sam, fashioned after local legend Dan Rice. Call (814) 774–3535 for more details.

- Mid-August, you can participate in *We Love Erie Days* on Perry Square in Erie. Call (814) 454–7191.

- Each August, the best of the West come East for the *North Washington Rodeo.* Sanctioned by the Professional Rodeo Cowboys and the Women's Professional Rodeo Association, the rodeo features standard categories—bareback bronco riding, calf roping, saddle bronco riding, steer wrestling, Brahma bull riding, and barrel racing—and specialty acts. Evening performances begin at 8:00 P.M. daily, rain or shine. Refreshments are

available. Admission is $9.00 for adults. For additional information call (724) 894–2968 or (724) 894–2050. The North Washington Rodeo is located on Route 38, 11 miles south of exit 5 of I-80.

- Late September, participate in the *Wine Country Harvest Festival* in Gravel Pit Park, North East. Call (724) 725–4262.

- During the third week of September in Tidioute (rhymes with pretty suit), you can participate in the *Pennsylvania State Championship Fishing Tournament.* Call the Warren County Tourism/ Northern Alleghenies Vacation Region at (800) 624–7802 for rules and regulations.

- Kids love the gremlins and goblins at the *Zoo Boo,* a scary evening event held for several weeks prior to Halloween. Call the Erie Zoo at (724) 864–4091.

- A bright name for a bright event: *Zoo-lumination,* held the last few weeks of December. Call the Erie Zoo at (724) 864–4091.

when the oil business fell off. A visitors center contains a pictorial history and artifacts of Pithole. By far the most interesting activity is wandering across the site of the town, where people and businesses used to thrive and where nothing remains but cellar holes, wells, and the depressions that used to be streets. You can pick up a walking-tour brochure at the visitors center, open from Memorial Day to Labor Day; Wednesday, noon to 5:00 P.M.; Thursday to Sunday, 10:00 A.M. to 5:00 P.M. Hours are subject to change, and modest fees are charged. Call (814) 589–7912 for more information.

Another way to see oil country and its history is to ride the *Oil Creek and Titusville Railroad*, sponsored by the *Oil Creek Railway Historical Society*. The two-hour trip runs from Titusville to Rynd Farm, 4 miles north of Oil City, passing through the sites of several boomtowns and some lovely countryside. You can board at the Drake Well Museum, at the Perry Street Station in Titusville, or at Rynd Farm. The schedule of northbound and southbound trains is complicated, may change without notice, and includes additional trains scheduled for special celebration weeks in the summer; moreover, you need advance tickets to guarantee a place on the train. To learn what the schedule will be when you plan to visit, write to the railroad at P.O. Box 68, Oil City 16301, or call (814) 827–2797 or (814) 676–1733. Ticket prices are moderately high.

If you'd like to make part of the same trip on bicycle, try the 10-mile paved trail along Oil Creek from Petroleum Center to Drake Well Park. The trail is open from 8:00 A.M. to dark.

Enjoy a more amusing kind of history at the *DeBence Antique Music Museum* (1261 Liberty Street) not far away on Route 8, 2 miles south of Franklin. The museum has more than one hundred antique music machines from the Gay Nineties and the Roaring Twenties. Hear the nickelodeons, band organs, orchestrions, and music boxes. The museum is open year-round, Tuesday to Saturday, 10:00 A.M. to 5:00 P.M.; Sunday, 12:30 to 5:00 P.M. Call (814) 432–5668 for details; a moderate admission fee is charged. Sounds great!

In downtown Franklin you can return to the railroad theme. The *Franklin Depot* (1215 Railroad Street) serves breakfast, lunch, dinner, and Sunday brunch in a rambling edifice consisting of an old train station and train cars. The kitchen used to be a baggage car. The waiting area and a dining room are in the original depot, which was built in 1866. Old dining cars brought in from the New York Central Railroad form the center of more dining rooms. The decor includes a chandelier from Oil City, the potbellied stove from a

DeBence Antique Music Museum

caboose, and full-size mannequins in old train uniforms. The restaurant, established in 1985, is open Monday through Friday, 9:00 A.M. to 8:00 P.M.; Saturday and Sunday, 7:00 A.M. to 8:00 P.M. or later. Phone (814) 437–1866.

The town of Franklin dates to 1753, when the French established Fort Machault here. Seven years later the British built Fort Venango. But, as with so much of this part of Pennsylvania, striking oil was what really gave life to the community. Take the time to check out the local-history displays in the *Hoge-Osmer House* (corner of South Park and Elk Streets) and at the *Venango County Courthouse* (Twelfth and Liberty Streets). If you're on Twelfth Street on Wednesday or Saturday, you can browse through the local farmers' market. You can wander around town, or you can request a self-guided walking tour at the Franklin Area Chamber of Commerce (1259 Liberty Street). For further information phone (814) 432–5823.

National Forest

The 500,000-acre **Allegheny National Forest of Pennsylvania** is one of fifteen national forests in the eastern United States and the only national forest in Pennsylvania. Hardwoods—black cherry, yellow poplar, white ash, red maple, and sugar maple—make up most of the timber. More than 65 million board feet of timber, especially black cherry, are harvested each year. The black cherry is used for fine furniture; much of the rest is used for pulpwood. **Hearts Content**, one comparatively small area of the forestland, has some of the oldest tracts of virgin beech and hemlock trees in the eastern United States.

- *The town of Corydon, near Warren, was submerged when the Kinzua Dam was built in 1965. But during a drought late in 1998, roads, bridges, and the foundations of buildings began peeking above the surface. Now that things have dried out, take a tour of the dam.*

- *The Kinzua Bridge, which dates to 1882, is the second-highest bridge in the United States today.*

You can access the forest from many points along Route 6 and Route 62 for some truly off-the-beaten-path travel. Just past East Hickory, at Endeavor, turn right on Route 666, heading into the forest. At Truemans you come to **Fools Creek Store**, perched by the road, on a curve, surrounded with woods and gardens. Here proprietor Margaret M. Stamm keeps hours from noon to 5:00 P.M., Saturday and Sunday. You may find her, her sign says, by chance or by appointment the rest of the week at (814) 968–3788. Margaret sells kerosene lamps and other small antiques as well as crackers and cans of soup, presumably for hunters. She says she is in her eighties, though she doesn't look it. But when she gets to telling you stories about her life and family, you figure she must be. There's no way she could have fit so many events into a shorter lifetime.

You Can Meet the Nicest People

The phone machine at the Allegheny National Forest Vacation Bureau asks you to spell out your name, street, and city. I refused. I spelled my last name and street, but I told the machine I would not spell Philadelphia. When Charley Dach, director of the bureau, called back, he skipped "Hello" and just said, "I want to talk to the person who won't spell Philadelphia." We laughed, he gave me information, and then he sent a fax addressed to: Susan Perloff, Phyladephia (which he crossed out), Philledelfia (crossed out), Philedefia (crossed), the city with the broken bell. I laughed. You can meet the nicest people in Pennsylvania. I forgot to tell Charley that for two years I received hundreds of letters listing my hometown as Billadelphia.

Side Trip

- *Photograph a magnificent 8-mile loop in the Allegheny River at Brady's Bend in East Brady.*

- *Some historians consider the Riverside Inn in Cambridge Springs to be the world's first health spa. It was built in 1885.*

From here, turn around and drive back about ¼ mile, where you see a dirt Forest Service road just before Mayburg. Turn left here, on Robbs Creek Road, also known as Forest Highway 116. Drive on to Hearts Road (though the signs often disappear) and turn left again. In about 2 miles you'll come to **Hearts Content Recreation Area** in the Allegheny National Forest. From Hearts Content you can hike, camp, and picnic—you know, to your heart's content. Whatever you do, you must take the scenic walk marked by signs. It is short and easy, and it seems to invite meditation. Streams make light music. The old deciduous trees arch high above, letting through just enough blue sky and sunlight to nurture the carpet of ferns, which reach your knees. Pines and hemlocks, nature's original incense, perfume the air. The forest floor, softened with pine needles and leaves, absorbs enough sound to make the surroundings seem as quiet as a cathedral. A six-year-old child walking through the area for the first time caught its mystery by asking, "Are we inside or outside?"

The **Hickory Creek Wilderness,** all 8,570 acres of it, is next to the campground. No motorized equipment is allowed. An 11-mile hiking loop takes you through rolling terrain. You will probably see deer, small wildlife, and all kinds of birds.

You can find a smaller—much smaller—peaceful, tranquil natural area in **Clear Creek State Park** by heading north from Sigel on Route 36, then north on Route 949. Call (814) 752–2368 to reach the park office. Scenically located in Jefferson County's Clear Creek Valley, the park encompasses 1,200 acres, with another 10,000 acres of natural resources in the adjacent Kittanning State Forest. Highlight of the park is the outstanding, self-guided Ox Shoe Trail, which depicts logging practices of earlier years. The area is noted for its abundant wildlife, its hunting and fishing, and the breathtaking beauty of its mountain laurel, which blooms from mid-June to early July, peaking in late June. See if you—or your kids— can identify some mountain laurel, the state flower. The plant grows from 3 to 6 feet high on rocky, wooded slopes. Look for petals that form a nearly perfect pink or white pentagon.

You're quite near **Cook Forest State Park**, which, in 1994, earned a *National Geographic* listing as one of the nation's top-fifty state parks. One of the finest stands of virgin timber in the eastern part of the United States is located here, and the area has been designated a National

NORTHWESTERN PENNSYLVANIA

Natural Landmark. The trees in this ancient forest are hundreds of years old, measuring up to 5 feet in diameter and towering nearly 200 feet. During a recent old-growth forest conference, three of the tallest trees in the East were identified here in Cook Forest. The old Cook sawmill, home to the Sawmill Center for the Arts, features summer theater, festivals, and craft markets and draws artisans to instruct classes in traditional arts and crafts. Much of the area exists almost as it was in the days of William Penn, when it was known as the Black Forest. Cecil B. DeMille used the park in his film *Unconquered*, starring Gary Cooper.

You're just minutes from historic Victorian Brookville, which is listed on the National Register of Historic Towns and which is the smallest community in the nation to have a full-service YMCA. In the tourist office at 175 Main Street, you can pick up a self-guided walking tour, showing the enchantments of this ninety-acre historic site. During the Dickensian Christmas celebration, sleigh bells ring and carolers sing. Do drop by.

In these parts you may hear a clarion call to slow down and smell the roses—or look at the leaves. Clarion, calling itself the autumn-leaf capital of the known world, boasts the rugged beauty of untamed natural resources and the nostalgia of an old-fashioned Main Street. It is unmistakably off the beaten path. Stop in the Free Library, on Main Street next to the post office, in downtown Clarion to pick up a booklet outlining an historical and architectural tour of Clarion, noting forty structures of interest. Enjoy the old-fashioned street lights, new sidewalks, and nostalgic building facades as you stroll downtown. A parasol would be nice.

PLACES TO STAY IN NORTHWESTERN PENNSYLVANIA

CLARION
Clarion House Bed & Breakfast, 77 South Seventh Avenue; (814) 226–4996 or (800) 416–3297.

COOKSBURG
Gateway Lodge, Cook Forest, Box 125, Route 36; (814) 744–8017.

ERIE
Spencer House Bed & Breakfast, 519 West Sixth Street; (814) 454–5984.

MERCER
Magoffin Inn, 129 South Pitt Street; (800) 841–0824.

WATTSBURG
Timbermist, 11050 Backus Road, Box 16442; (814) 739–2296 or (888) 739–9004.

**PLACES TO EAT IN
NORTHWESTERN
PENNSYLVANIA**

BROOKVILLE
Plyler's Pizza and Family
Restaurant, Routes 28,
322 and 36;
(814) 849–7357.

CLARION
Clarion Clipper, Route 68,
half-mile north of I-80;
(814) 226–7950.

ERIE
Smuggler's Wharf,
3 State Street;
(814) 459–4273.
On Lake Erie.

Rum Runners,
133 East Dobbins Landing;
(814) 455–4292. On Lake
Erie, with dock space
available.

SHARON
Quaker Steak & Lube,
101 Chestnut Street;
(724) 981–9464 or
(800) 468–9464. Located in
a former gas station. Your
dining companions are a
1936 Chevrolet on a grease
rack and a Corvette sus-
pended from the ceiling.
Hot wings and cool cars.

TIONESTA
Five Forks Restaurant,
Route 62, 1 1/2 miles off
Tionesta; (814) 755–2455.
Overlooking the Allegheny
River.

North Central Pennsylvania: Allegheny National Forest

Wild Country

ot a light? Whether your answer is "no," "yes, but it's broken," or "what are you talking about," you can start your wild-country trek with a fiery sight-seeing experience—by visiting the ***Zippo Visitors Center*** (Zippo Drive) in Bradford, on Route 219 just below the New York border. Zippo was the company that first made windproof lighters. (Tradition says that zippers had recently been invented, and the inventor liked the name, so he copied it.) Your visit includes the museum, which opened in 1994, the repair shop, and the gift shop (though not the factory). Since Zippos include a lifetime guarantee, and since the repair shop receives about 400 lighters daily, there's always something to watch. The center is open Sunday, noon to 4:00 P.M.; other days, 9:00 A.M. to 5:00 P.M. Look for streetlights shaped like giant lighters. Call (814) 368–2863 or (888) 442–1932.

Next stop is an otherworldly place—the closest Pennsylvania comes to Antarctica. It's hard to believe, but it's legit—an ***ice mine***, a quirk of nature that keeps water frozen year-round. It's in Smethport, at the intersection of Route 59 and Route 6, between Warren and Bradford. From the parking lot, walk down the stone steps, transplanted from houses in Kinzua before that town was flooded to create the reservoir. ("We pronounce it *kin-zoo*," says Charley Dach, executive director of the Allegheny National Forest Vacation Bureau. "The 'A' is silent. Tourists call it *kin-zoo-a*;

> ### Trivia
>
> *In Austin, just south of Route 6 on Route 872, a dam broke in 1911, leveling two towns and killing eighty-nine people. The site is listed on the National Register of Historic Places.*

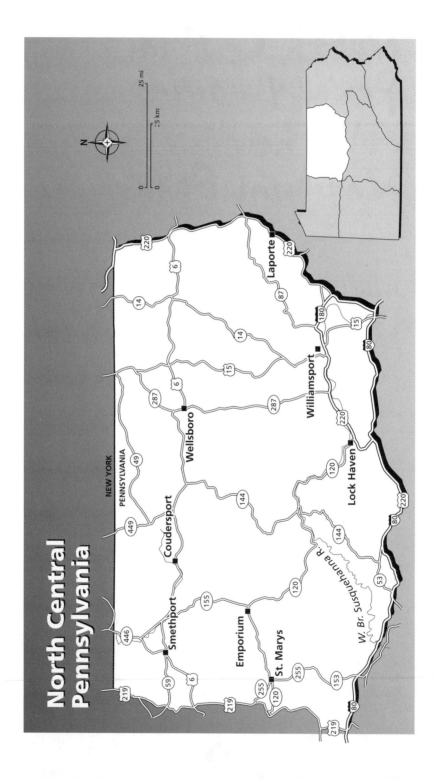

North Central Pennsylvania

AUTHOR'S TOP TEN FAVORITES IN NORTH CENTRAL PENNSYLVANIA

Elk

Frenchville

Grand Canyon of Pennsylvania

Little League Baseball Museum

Lookout Tower (which we climbed at Valley Forge)

The Slide—watching, not riding

Wellsboro

Woolrich Factory Store

World Series of Little League Baseball

World's End State Park

that's how we can tell who's a tourist—if we can't tell you're a tourist because you're driving a new car.") As you descend, on your right is a big rock. How big? Very big—3$\frac{1}{2}$ stories tall and more than 300 feet long. Legend says that early Native Americans huddled behind the rock to find shelter from storms. On your left is the ice mine. Stand within 10 feet, and you can feel the chill—below thirty-four degrees, even in summer. People get ice from it year-round, says Dach, and the ice, like the admission, is free. "Every once in a while, in the summer, a big guy goes in and gets stuck; we have to lard him up to get him out."

Pop up to **Singer's Country Store** (814–368–6151) at the crossroads that is Custer City, at the intersection of Route 219 and Route 770. For about sixty cents you can pluck a fresh pickle out of the briny barrel and chat about the countryside with the owner, Mary Dach (yes, she's related). (The vendor who has supplied pickles to Singer's for more than fifty years is training her great-granddaughter in the fine points of pickling, so the supply should be constant for the next few decades.)

Head east on Route 6, through Coudersport. Across from Denton Hill State Park at Galeton, you reach the **Pennsylvania Lumber Museum**, an outdoor gallery that depicts the history and technology of Pennsylvania's prosperous lumbering activities. A century ago white pine and hemlock were the wealth of this nation. Two of the world's largest sawmills were located in Austin (24 miles southwest of the museum) and Galeton (11 miles southeast). The museum displays more than 3,000 artifacts related to the logging industry. Walk among the old buildings of the logging camp, sawmill, and a logging pond, all surrounded by Appalachian Mountain wilderness. The visit recreates the tough life for the woods workers, or "wood hicks," in the days of

For the Birds

Enjoy Tioga-Hammond and Cowanesque Lakes, where wildlife is protected and recreational opportunities abound. Check out the osprey habitat.

lumbering. The men worked six days a week, from 5:00 A.M. to 9:00 P.M. (no, that's not a typo!) with time off for extended periods of downpour, though rarely for cold or snow. In about 1910 the workweek was reduced to six ten-hour days, and in 1920 to five eight-hour days. Lice and dirt were everywhere. Bathing facilities were nowhere.

Even though the workers' conditions weren't pristine, the forests and trees were, and the giant white pines were in great demand. Wood hicks felled the trees, tied them into rafts, and floated them down the Susquehanna River and into the Chesapeake Bay, where they were exported to England to be made into ships. The world's best timber for boat spars came from the Galeton region; it was not uncommon to find 100-foot-long spars with the small end a foot in diameter—spars that were born and raised in north-central Pennsylvania. The Lumber Museum, administered by the Pennsylvania Historical and Museum Commission, is open 9:00 A.M. to 5:00 P.M. daily in spring, summer, and fall. Winter hours vary; closed major holidays. Admission fee is modest. Phone (814) 435-2652, fax (814) 435-6361, or write for more information to P.O. Box 239, 5660 US Route 6, Galeton 16922.

Trivia
Pennsylvania leads the nation in producing mushrooms and potato chips.

The most dramatic aspect of this section of the state is the mountainous and wooded **Pine Creek Gorge**, commonly known as the **Grand Canyon of Pennsylvania**. The gorge, comprising mostly state parks and wilderness, is 50 miles long and 1,000 feet deep, covering 300,000 acres of state forest. You can access the canyon by driving south on Route 660, midway between Galeton and Wellsboro.

In the good old days, before Shakespeare wrote about Hamlet and before the pharaohs built the pyramids, the headwaters of Pine Creek, near Ansonia, flowed to the northeast. Then came glaciers. As the glacial ice melted, it left a dam of gravel, sand, and clay, which blocked the creek's path. This natural dam forced Pine Creek to reverse direction and flow south. Thus formed the Grand Canyon, with land formations dating back over 350 million years. And grand it is. In 1968 the National Park Service declared a 12-mile section a National Natural Landmark.

At two state parks — **Leonard Harrison State Park** on the east rim of the canyon and **Colton Point State Park** on the west (570-724-3061 reaches both park offices)—you can stop at lookouts and pick up short hiking trails that don't require safari gear. Leonard Harrison State Park has a nature center (open summer and fall) and a relatively easy trail along the rim that gives you an orientation to the canyon. If you follow Turkey Path about a mile down to Pine Creek, you'll encounter more ambitious hikes that take in creeks and waterfalls. The area is noted for ferns, songbirds, and superb scenery in any season. Leonard Harrison, a Wellsboro businessman who contributed time and money to the community, donated much of this land before his death in 1929.

NORTH CENTRAL PENNSYLVANIA

Trivia

In 1892, the first lighted nighttime football game was played at Mansfield University, Mansfield.

In Colton Point State Park you can hike an easy mile-long loop through a hardwood forest rich in wildflowers and fragrant mountain laurel, the state flower. Henry Colton was a lumberman who supervised the harvesting of trees in the area in the late 1800s. Most people visit the Grand Canyon of Pennsylvania in the fall for the foliage, but spring is also splendid, especially if you prefer greater privacy. Winter offers cross-country skiing and snowmobiling.

Wellsboro, the Tioga County seat, is a beautiful little town, with old trees and gaslights lining the streets. In the public square, called the Green, a fountain splashes over a statue of Wynken, Blynken, and Nod in their wooden shoe. When Wellsboro was incorporated in 1830, it had 250 residents. In the 1990 census, it had grown to 3,400, with another five thousand within a radius of 5 miles and five thousand more within 10 miles.

The *Penn Wells Dining Room* features a Saturday smorgasbord and a Sunday brunch in addition to moderately priced luncheons and dinners. Call (570) 724–2111 or fax (570) 724–3703 for hotel and dining information. A block away, the *Penn Wells Lodge* (570–724–3463) has more modern facilities, including an indoor swimming pool, exercise room, and sauna. Reach the dining room or lodge at (800) 545–2446.

You can request an area map from the Wellsboro Chamber of Commerce, P.O. Box 733, 114 Main Street, Wellsboro 16901. Phone (570) 724–1926 or fax (570) 724–5084.

Pennsylvania Town Names We Like

*T*hirsty? *Follow I–80 to get to Stillwater (exit 36) and Swiftwater (exit 44).*

- **Monarchy.** *Who says Americans don't believe in the monarchy? We have a* King of Prussia, *now home of one of the country's largest megamalls; plus a town named* Queen, *a* Princeton *and a* Duke Center.

- **Upper class.** *Visit communities named Upper Darby, Upper Merion, Upper Black Eddy, and Upper Strasburg. Plus Upland, Topton, Highland, and Highspire.*

- **What's in a name?** *Philadelphia International Airport is in Essington, Harrisburg Airport is in Middletown, and Pittsburgh International is in Coraopolis.*

- **Law firm name we'd like to see.** *Clayton, Drayton, and Creighton.*

The End of the World

Another near-wilderness park is **World's End State Park**, as remote as it sounds. To get there take Route 220 to Eagles Mere, which is about midpoint between Route 6 and I–80, then go west on Route 154. Part of the lure of World's End is its primitive quality and its ideal position for picnicking, fishing, swimming, and boating. The park phone number is (570) 924-3287.

The town of Eagles Mere, which used to call itself "the town that time forgot," is so lovely and simple that it might have inspired Norman Rockwell. In the 1800s wealthy folks from the Main Line outside Philadelphia visited the 2,100-foot-high mountain area, fell in love with the clean air and clear water, and set about developing the area. They built Victorian "cottages," similar to the gargantuan dwellings of the same name in Newport, Rhode Island—cottages that would sleep thirty-four of your closest friends without resorting to futons.

While the geology is a nature photographer's utopia, one human-made element also stands out. It's the **Slide**, a toboggan run built in 1904. When the first intrepid rider, sitting on a big iron shovel, tested the grooved, planed, wooden course, he whizzed so fast that he burned the seat off his pants. Today the slide is a 120-ton, 1,200-foot-long channel of ice, down which you can ride in relative safety—if you first pay a few bucks and sign a waiver—at 45 miles per hour.

Trivia Tidbits

• So what if Abe Lincoln didn't sleep in Wellsboro. That's no reason not to claim his presence. Or presents. At 140 Main Street is the Lincoln Door House. Abraham Lincoln gave the door—now bright red—to Dr. and Mrs. J. H. Shearer when they bought the house in 1858. Mrs. Shearer and Mrs. Lincoln were girlfriends in Springfield, Illinois.

• Guidebooks say the name Tioga comes from an old Indian word, but they disagree on what that word meant. Some say it meant the meeting of two rivers, and others say it meant gateway or place to enter. Either way, Tioga County is a hunter's paradise, serving as home to many species of white-tailed deer, bear, cottontail rabbits, wild turkey, ruffed grouse, and ducks.

• Between 1628 and 1762, three kings of England issued four separate charters giving land in today's Tioga County to three different states— once to Pennsylvania, once to Massachusetts, and twice to Connecticut. The Continental Congress resolved state ownership in 1780. It's part of the Keystone State. For now.

The Tower that Traveled

The **Lookout Tower** *in Leonard Harrison State Park affords views for 100 miles with the naked eye. The tower originally stood atop Mount Joy, in Valley Forge, where George Washington and his troops spent the winter of 1776 and 1777. Built in 1906, the tower was a birders' haven until 1988, when surrounding trees grew too tall for its use in observation. At that time, it traveled 240 miles to its present home. Visit the tower daily, sunrise to sunset, weather permitting. Climb 125 steps to reach the top.*

To relax after this thrilling plummet, treat yourself to dinner at the **Eagles Mere Inn**, the last remaining full-service inn from the nineteenth century. Its cozy guest rooms make you yearn for the days before pocket pagers. In the dining room, where lace covers the tables, hosts Susan and Peter Glaubitz provide a menu that changes daily but always reflects Peter's substantial background as a chef. One night you might try cajun steak; another, baby French hen in cranberry Merlot sauce; and a third, trout stuffed with sole and shiitake mousseline. If you prefer vegetarian or other special diets, call ahead (570) 525–3273 or (800) 426–3273, or visit www.eaglesmereinn.com, and they'll try to honor your request. Write to the inn at Mary Avenue, Box 356, Eagles Mere 17731.

Like hot dogs? Like peanuts and Cracker Jack? Every summer, **Williamsport** hosts the Little League World Series, attracting thousands of spectators and some of the best twelve-year-old baseball players in the world. The thwack (or, perhaps, the ping) of the bat and the shouts of the kids remind you why the sport is the national pastime. The **Little League Baseball Museum** (570–326–3607) honors Tom Selleck, Dan Quayle ("Does *shortstop* have an *e*?"), Kareem Abdul-Jabbar, Nolan Ryan, and Mike Schmidt, to name a few. Admission costs $5.00 per adult. Summer hours are Monday through Saturday, 9:00 A.M. to 7:00 P.M.; Sunday, noon to 7:00 P.M. The rest of the year, it closes two hours earlier. Open daily except Thanksgiving, Christmas, and New Year's Day. Located on Route 6, Williamsport.

Just north of Route 220, between Lock Haven and Williamsport, is the town of Woolrich. If the name sounds familiar, look inside the neckband of your hunting jacket. The company of Woolrich, in the town of Woolrich, makes sportswear and outerwear under both its own brand and that of other companies, including L. L. Bean and Lands End. John Rich built his first woolen mill on Plum Run in 1830, and the rest, as they say, is red buffalo plaid. The actors in *The Horse Whisperer* wore Woolrich garb. Visit the original factory outlet store in Woolrich (570–769–7401) or at outlet malls in Grove City, Lancaster, and Reading. Visit the Woolrich Company Store from 9:00 A.M. to 6:00 P.M., Monday to Thursday; 9:00 A.M. to 9:00 P.M., Friday and Saturday; and noon to 5:00 P.M. on Sunday. Seventeen other states have outlets of these made-in-Pennsylvania garments.

One treasure in this neck of the northern woods is the 23,000-acre **Bucktail State Park**, which extends southeast—and downstream—from Emporium to Lock Haven. Route 120, a good road between the mountains, essentially parallels the park, as does the Susquehanna River for half the distance. This pleasant, scenic drive takes you through state forests, parks, and wild areas. If you're in the mood for a more active experience, hike a trail or choose a private clearing for a view and a picnic. Almost always, you can count on being alone. Incidentally, the park's name comes only indirectly from the deer of the same name; the name actually commemorates a troop of local woodsmen who called themselves the Bucktail Regiment when they served in the Civil War.

West of Emporium is St. Marys, a town with a moist claim to fame—**Straub Brewery**, (303 Sorg Street). Straub's is one of the smallest independent breweries left in the United States. "Of course, that depends on how you define 'small,' " says owner Terry Straub. "A microbrewery makes less than 15,000 barrels per year and sells it only on the premises.

Pass Me a Wafer, Please

*I*f you live in Montgomery, Alabama; Madras, Oregon; or anywhere in between, Pennsylvania has an effect on your cookies. The packages of saltines, chocolate-chip cookies, and buttered biscuits that you buy near home may be marked REG. PENNA. DEPT. AGRICULTURE *even if they were made in Madrid, Spain, or Minneapolis, Minnesota. Why? Because the Pennsylvania*

Department of Agriculture has the strictest standards in the country for packaged baked goods. The department inspects all Pennsylvania bakeries and requires copies of inspection reports for out-of-state and out-of-country bakeries that want to sell to Pennsylvanians. REG. PENNA. DEPT. AGRICULTURE indicates to oatmeal-cookie lovers everywhere that the package comes from a sanitary, safe facility.

We made 35,000 barrels in 1998, and we distribute it in Pennsylvania and Ohio. So it's okay to call us '*one of* the smallest.' " Bottoms up. Straub produces beer made of water, malt, grains, and hops; no sugar, syrup; or additives. The *Connoisseur's Guide to Beer* named Straub's one of the five best-tasting beers in the country. The company distributes only within a radius of 150 miles, which means that to taste the beer, you must either visit the area or entice a friend to send you a six-pack. St. Marys is where Routes 255 and 120 intersect. Hours are Monday through Friday, 9:00 A.M. to noon for free tours and free tastings from Straub's "eternal tap." To be sure you catch the brewery in operation, call (814) 834–2875 and hope to be placed on hold: The recording plays the sound of a tinkling brook, a subtle reminder of the all-fresh ingredients. Visit the Web site at www.straubbeer.com.

If you want to see something strikingly singular, head west on Route 120, sometimes called Elk View Drive, toward Ridgway and keep your eyes peeled for elk, more than 300 of them. This is the only wild, free-roaming herd of elk east of the Mississippi. The St. Marys airport and the village of Benezette, on Route 555, are prime viewing spots.

Most of the mature bull elk live near St. Marys, except during the September/October rutting season, when they travel about 9 miles south to join the cows near Benezette. (Some guys will do anything, it seems.)

Ski Areas Off the Beaten Path

I got him to marry me, so I don't have to ski anymore. He proposed on chairlift six, on a mountain in another time zone. The following day I skied with former President Gerald Ford and placed last in a ski race, earning the "snow snail" award. I hung up my skis. Nonetheless, skiing is part of the family culture. A few years ago, to win a bet, Ed skied one run at each of six Pocono ski areas in one day. I drove getaway. If you're in Pennsylvania to ski, you know the biggest resorts. Of the twenty-five areas listed in the White Book of Skiing, here are the seven smallest, each with less than 500 feet vertical drop.

Blue Marsh, *Bernville;* (610) 488-7412.

Crystal Lake, *Hughesville;* (717) 584-2698.

Mt. Pleasant, *Cambridge Springs;* (814) 734-1641.

Mount Tone, *Lake Como;* (717) 842-2544.

Mystic Mountain, *Farmington;* (412) 329-6979.

Resort at Split Rock, *Lake Harmony;* (580) 722-9111.

Tussey Mountain, *Boalsburg;* (814) 466-6810 or (800) 733-2754.

Rutting season is when you might hear them bugling, if you're lucky. The royal and imperial bull elk, which can weigh up to a thousand pounds, sport twelve-point and fourteen-point antlers, respectively. The racks on older bucks may spread up to 5 feet in length. Speaking of respect, keep a respectful—and safe—distance away. Bring cameras, camcorders, and microphones, but no guns. Best viewing times are early morning and just before dusk.

Frenchville used to be a place where you could go to *parler français*, but no longer. Mary Kay Royer, a seventh-generation Frenchviller, tells the story. Early in the 1800s a Philadelphia lawyer acquired a tract of land in upstate Pennsylvania. He advertised it in French newspapers at the bargain rate of twelve acres free with each fifty paid. And he found buyers. "You'll notice," says Royer, "that everyone came from within about 20 miles of one another, from Normandy and Picardy in France." Men pioneered, she says, apparently walking overland from the ports of Baltimore and New York. When they signed their purchase agreements, they didn't understand that they were buying isolated land inaccessible by normal transport. Clearfield, which was just developing, was the closest town, and Bellefonte was next closest—yet neither of those was (or is) a thriving metropolis. Eventually the men sent home for their families.

Elk Lore

*J*une is the most popular month for elk to have babies.

Female elk, or cows, usually hang out with the other ladies, disappearing for privacy a few days before childbirth. Mommy and baby remain solitary for about three weeks.

In late summer, the bull elk's antlers are usually white and ivory; they darken later as the animal rubs against shrubs and trees covered with juices and sap.

Elk antlers, which can grow a half-inch a day, are among the fastest-growing animal tissues.

Elk, like many humans, dislike thunderstorms.

During the rutting season, males mate with as many cows as possible, act dangerous to scare off other males, and feed and rest very little. They may lose a hundred pounds in a month. That's serious rutting.

Best Annual Events in North Central Pennsylvania

- Every sunny day, you can catch a perfect sunrise from **Colton Point State Park.** Enjoy the sunset from **Leonard Harrison State Park.** Both times, you luxuriate in a view of the Grand Canyon of Pennsylvania.

- During the third weekend in February, the Mosquito Creek Sportsmen's Club, Frenchville, holds its **Coyote Hunt.** Every state has coyotes, says member Ray Saville, and they're the smartest animals in the woods. Must be, because, during the 1999 hunt, when 3,880 hunters paid their $5.00 membership fee and additional hunting fee, they caught only twenty-one coyotes. To learn more, fax the club at (814) 263–4559. To reach a human, call weekends at (814) 263–4510, or write Box 218, Frenchville 16836.

- **Mary Wells Days,** a founder's day celebration, takes place over Memorial Day in Wellsboro. Call (570) 724–1926 for details.

- First weekend in June, you can watch the **Susquehannock Trail Pro** auto racing rally in Wellsboro. Call (570) 724–1926 for details.

- Third weekend in June, Wellsboro holds the **Pennsylvania State Laurel Festival.** The parade is on Saturday. Call (570) 724–1926 for details.

- Celebrate **Fourth of July** weekend in Mansfield. Call the Mansfield Chamber of Commerce at (570) 662–3442. Or celebrate the Fourth in Galeton, where thousands of visitors watch the fire-

works in the natural amphitheater. Call (814) 435–2321 for details.

- First weekend in October you can come home to the **Homecoming Harvest** in Wellsboro. Expect sidewalk sales, craft and food vendors, and antiques. Call (570) 724–1926 for details.

- Watch the **World Series of Little League Baseball** in Williamsport during the last full week of August that does not include the Saturday before Labor Day. If you go in 2000, you'll see the four top U.S. teams (from the East, Central, West, and South regions) compete against the four best international teams (from Canada, Latin America, the Far East, and Europe). If you go in 2001 or later, you'll see eight versus eight teams. Seats are free, and the only day you need a ticket is the Saturday of the championship, since the stadium holds *only* about 5,000 people. The stadium is built into a hillside, so the other 30,000 or 40,000 spectators without tickets spend the day picnicking on the hill and watching from afar. For tickets, write *in January* to the Little League Museum, P. O. Box 3485, Williamsport 17701. Mark the envelope World Series Tickets. Go, Babe! For more information call (570) 326–3607.

- *1890s Weekend,* last weekend in September. Call the Mansfield Chamber of Commerce at (570) 662–3442.

- First Saturday in December, catch the **Dickens of a Christmas** in Wellsboro. Call (570) 724–1926 for details.

In this isolated area, settled in 1832, people farmed, mined, and worked on the developing railroads. When townsmen logged, they rode downstream speaking French. They stuck together, speaking French among themselves and mastering the smidgen of English necessary to communicate with outsiders. Even the inscriptions on tombstones are in French, though misspelled and grammatically incorrect. As new inventions came along—automobile, radio, television—the villagers incorporated English words into their talk. The few people in Frenchville who are still fluent in French speak a classically pure French, without an American accent and *sans* the slang of contemporary French streets. But few French-speakers remain. Royer's father, now 65, spoke French at home as a child but was prohibited from speaking it once he got to school, as were others of his generation. He's lost the French he once knew. Both Royer's parents grew up in Frenchville—"almost everybody is related somehow. And we don't get many newcomers. You can live here ten years and still be the new person on the block."

The village of several hundred people hides in a pocket of hills and rugged woodlands in Clearfield County. The trip over pitted blacktop roads winds through the remains of played-out strip mines, some of them growing scraggly conifers planted as part of reclamation projects. The heart of the community, as always, is St. Mary's Church, a parish established in 1840. Its first home was a log cabin, where the cemetery now stands. The current building, of native hand-cut stone, was occupied in 1870, the year the town's picnic originated. It was a ceremony of thanks for the construction of the church, and it continues annually, during the third weekend in July, in recognition of that heritage. For more information about Frenchville, St. Marys, or the thanksgiving celebration, e-mail stmary@vicon.net, or phone the rectory at (814) 263–4354.

PLACES TO STAY IN NORTH CENTRAL PENNSYLVANIA

COUDERSPORT
Potato City Country Inn, Route 6; (814) 274–7133; fax (814) 274–7135.

FRENCHVILLE
Coudriet House Inn Bed & Breakfast, Route 879; (814) 263–4666.

GALETON
Ox Yoke Motel and Restaurant, R.D. 1, Box 174; (814) 435–6522.

KNOXVILLE
Woods Bed and Breakfast, R. R. 1, Box 818; (570) 376–3711.

RIDGWAY
Towers Victorian Inn, 330 South Street; (814) 772–7657; www.ncentral.com/~towers.

ST. MARYS
Towne House Inn, 138 Center Street; (814) 781–1556 or (800) 851–9180; www.shopstmarys.com.

WELLSBORO
Canyon Motel, 18 East
Avenue; (570) 724–1681 or
(800) 255–2718.

Coach Stop Inn, Route 6,
R.R. #4, Box 137;
(570) 724–5361 or
(800) 829–4130;
fax (570) 724–7773.

**PLACES TO EAT IN
NORTH CENTRAL
PENNSYLVANIA**

ST. MARYS
Bavarian Inn, 33 South St.
Marys Street;
(814) 834–2161.

New Peacock, 2 Shawmut
Square; (814) 834–2788.

Station Inn, 322 Depot
Street; (814) 834–1010.

WELLSBORO
Antlers, Route 6 West;
(814) 435–6300.

Log Cabin, Route 6;
(814) 435–8808.

Steak House, 27 Main
Street; (570) 724–9092.
Closed Sunday.

Northeastern Pennsylvania: Pocono Mountains and Endless Mountains

You could start a visit to Northeastern Pennsylvania in **Promised Land State Park**, but where could you go next? Well, just about anywhere, really, but it might be a letdown. Moses, after all, didn't go from the Promised Land back to Egypt, did he? And if you *start* at the end of the world, what's your destination, over the rainbow? (If you're a glass-is-half-full type, you could start in Archbold Pothole State Park.)

Hard-Coal Country

To understand Northeastern Pennsylvania, you need to understand coal mining. Legend says that in 1791 in the quiet village of Summit Hill, in western Carbon County, Pennsylvania, a major discovery altered American history. While tracking game, a hardy backwoodsman named Philip Ginder accidentally kicked a piece of shiny, black rock. He pocketed the stone and took it to Revolutionary War veteran Colonel Jacob Weiss, who took it to his colleagues in Philadelphia. Turns out, Ginder had discovered anthracite coal, often called "black diamonds" because of its value in the marketplace.

As you probably learned in elementary school, coal is a fuel substance composed of plant material. You can inspect primitive forms of coal if you fail to rake leaves in your backyard for a few thousand years. The two primary types of coal are anthracite, or hard coal, and bituminous, or soft coal. Anthracite is more valuable because it has more carbon content and less moisture and thus it burns cleaner.

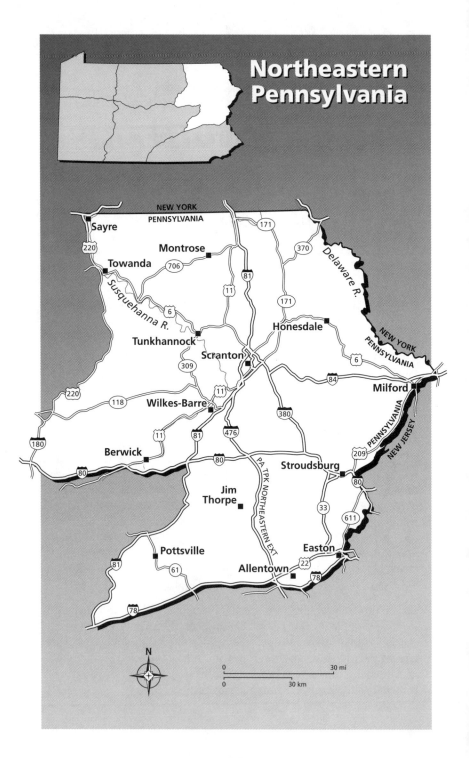

Northeastern Pennsylvania

NORTHEASTERN PENNSYLVANIA

AUTHOR'S TOP TEN FAVORITES IN NORTHEASTERN PENNSYLVANIA

Blue Mountain Sports

Boulder Field at Hickory Run State Park

Delaware Water Gap National Recreation Area

French Azilum

Inn at Jim Thorpe

Jim Thorpe

Mountainhome Diner

Roebling Bridge

Ryah House

Upper Mill

In the coal region, some stretches of roadway through the hills are lovely, though the landscape has been marred by coal mining. The working mines aren't especially aesthetically pleasing, but the area is historically rich in the details that let us see how people there used to live and work. It makes for an interesting visit.

Nowhere is the legacy of coal mining more obvious than in Scranton. In downtown Scranton, on Cedar Avenue between Lackawanna Avenue and Moosic Street, the ***Pennsylvania Anthracite Heritage Museum*** describes the lives and work of the ethnic communities in the region. Exhibits survey activities related to canals, railroads, silk mills, factories, and, of course, coal. The museum is on Bald Mountain Road in McDade Park. Take the North Scranton Expressway to the Keyser Avenue exit. Follow Keyser Avenue and signs to McDade Park. The museum is open 9:00 A.M. to 5:00 P.M., Monday through Saturday; noon to 5:00 P.M., Sunday; closed on major holidays. Admission fee is $3.50. Call (570) 963–4804.

Part of the same complex are the ***Scranton Iron Furnaces***, open daily from 8:00 A.M. to dusk. These four huge blast-furnace stacks, built by the Scranton brothers between 1841 and 1857, are remnants of the iron industry around which Scranton grew, with coal mining and railroads falling into place as companion industries. Admission is free.

McDade Park has picnic tables and barbecues, so you can grab a bite

Where's Throop?

*O*n a back road near Promised Land State Park, I'm lost. I stop a truck driver for directions and, while he studies my map, I notice his truck comes from Throop, Pennsylvania. "Where's Throop?" I ask.

"Troop," he says, not answering.

"Throop," I repeat.

"Troop," he says.

"Your truck says it's from Throop," I tell him.

"Well, it's up near Scranton," he says, wishing lady drivers were smarter. "But in Scranton, we don't pronounce our Hs. We say we have a 'rule of t'umb.' We say 't'rough,' not 'through,' and we have 't'ings,' not 'things.'"

Tanks.

before going on to the **Lackawanna Coal Mine** tour, which begins next to the Heritage Museum. The tour takes you down into an abandoned slope mine to see what the miners did and what conditions were like. An electrically powered coal car lowers you from the loading platform to the mine interior. The big, new yellow car and hoist were designed especially for this purpose.

Inside the mine, a retired miner or teacher takes you on a 600-foot tour along a wooden walkway, explaining the sights and answering questions. In the spacious underground area, mannequins in mining clothes and a life-sized stuffed mule seem to say, "Hi." Although the mine isn't really dirty, it *is* underground, and coal can leave its marks, so consider blue jeans and walking shoes. The hour-long tours leave hourly, more frequently during busy times. More exhibits and artifacts are housed above ground in a building called Shifting Shanty. From May through October, tours begin at 10:00 A.M.; the last tour leaves at 4:00 P.M. Admission is $6.00. Call (570) 963–6463.

Within walking distance of the mine is the **Steamtown National Historic Site**, the only place in the national park system that tells the story of steam railroading. The Steamtown Yard is open to the public. Visit the museum, which showcases coal-fired steam locomotives, restored cabooses, freight cars, and railroad coaches, offering a nostalgic journey to a period in American history when industry was on the move. The sights, sounds, smells, and even tastes of that era are brought to life in the presence of some of the most powerful machines ever built. It's located in the original Delaware, Lackawanna & Western Railroad Yard, which operated continuously from 1851 to 1963. The site boasts active locomotive and restoration shops and a complex that includes a visitors center, history and technology museums, a 250-seat theater, and an operating roundhouse and turntable, the device that was invented to let trains turn around and start over again in the other direction. It's open daily except Thanksgiving, Christmas, and New Year's Day. While you're here, ride the steam train, a scenic, two-hour, 26-mile round-trip to Moscow and back. (That's Moscow, Pennsylvania.) Reserve ahead for the trains, which run from late May until late October. The park is open daily from 9:00 A.M. to 5:00 P.M. (9:00 A.M. to 6:00 P.M. during the excursion season). Adults pay $7.00 for the museum and $10.00 for the train, or $15.00 for both. Although the entrance to the park is on Lackawanna Avenue, the mailing address is 150 South Washington Avenue, Scranton 18503. For more details, visit www.nps.gov/stea, or call (570) 340–5200 or (888) 693–9391; TDD (telecommunications device for the deaf) (717) 340–5207.

Magician Harry Houdini performed in Scranton, where the **Houdini Museum** (1433 North Main) honors his memory. Ehrich (or Erik) Weiss (or Weisz)—who, abracadabra, became Harry Houdini—was born in 1874 in Budapest and moved to the United States when he was four. He lived for years in Appleton, Wisconsin, of which he later said: "The greatest escape I ever made was when I left Appleton." In 1918, at the Hippodrome in New York City, Houdini first made an elephant disappear on stage. He performed underwater stunts, for which he practiced by holding his breath in the bathtub. In the museum you'll see Houdini's explanation of how he escaped from the incredible predicaments in which he put himself: "My brain is the key that sets me free." Since his parents spoke Yiddish, Hungarian, and German, his brain was probably also the key that taught him English.

The Houdini Museum also catalogs the history of Scranton and its coal and railroading industries. One exhibit, for instance, says that the Lackawanna Railroad created the image of Phoebe Snow, a delicate woman in a white dress, to foster the idea that riding coal-run trains was a clean event, hence the white dress. "Nothing could be further from the truth," it says. The old steam engines blew soot onto passengers riding the trains with open windows on warm days. Call (570) 342–5555.

Near Scranton is the **Dorflinger-Suydam Wildlife Sanctuary**, a 600-acre nature preserve and unique museum. The Dorflinger family manufactured glass until the 1920s, and eight U.S. presidents owned some of it. Today the museum of cut glass is open mid-May through October, 10:00 A.M. to 4:00 P.M., Wednesday through Saturday; 1:00 to 4:00 P.M. on Sunday. It's located on Route 6, midway between Hawley and Honesdale; the town is called White Mills, and the location is the intersection of Long Ridge Road and Elizabeth Street. Write to P. O. Box 356, White Mills 18473, or call (570) 253–1185 for more information.

Ricketts Glen

Knowledgeable outdoorspeople consider **Ricketts Glen** the most spectacular of Pennsylvania's state parks. Its more than 13,000 acres of mountains, streams, waterfalls, and lakes spread through Sullivan, Columbia, and Luzerne counties. The glen has twenty-two named waterfalls and a virgin hemlock forest with trees more than 500 years old. The only activity permitted in the natural area is walking. No picnics, campfires, camping, mountain biking, whining, or picking wildflowers. Just hiking. You'll find bass, a swimming beach, and a summer-only concession stand on Lake Jean. The park has 23 miles of hiking trails, some strictly for the physically fit and some shorter loops that are less strenuous. The Falls Trail along the gorge gives you a view of all the falls in the glen and is breathtakingly close to the edge. It is possible to find deserted hiking trails almost any time and wander into the woods feeling that you're the only person in the forest primeval.

The hills are alive with the sound of RVs. You can rent cabins at Ricketts Glen (though not in the natural areas), and the park has good camping for recreational vehicles and tents. Reservations are mandatory for overnight visits, especially during high season, which often lasts through October. Drive to Ricketts Glen via Route 487 or Route 118 north, depending on which side of the park you wish to enter. The grade is so steep that large vehicles should take Route 220, then turn north on Route 487 at Dushore. The park phone number is (570) 477–5675.

Working Valleys

From Scranton you can get to Hazleton quickly on I–81 or cross over to Route 11 and drive down along the Susquehanna. From about Wilkes Barre, the drive becomes especially hilly in the narrow river valley. Almost any time you tire of it, you can pick up a short road back to the interstate to Hazleton, another formerly thriving coal burgh that was founded in 1837. Whether you follow the highway or your own way, you'll pass some little river towns—not the picturesque, renovated towns of slick decorating magazines, but real working towns inhabited by laboring folks. You may still see women wearing babushkas (head scarves), kids scuffing their shoes on the sidewalks, and town merchants sitting in front of their stores during idle moments.

Nine miles east of Hazleton, the **Eckley Miners' Village** gives you a chance to visit a spot that is part historic site and part living community. It is authentic, not because it has been re-created, but because it has never has changed—the black silt heaps, open strip mines, and slag are ever present. Eckley was a company town from its settlement in 1854 until 1971. Now it's administered by the Pennsylvania Historical and Museum Commission; its population of retired miners, some widows, and children has dwindled to about fifteen persons. The village, covering a hundred acres, includes fifty-eight buildings with exhibits showing daily life for coal-mining families: first the English settlers, then Welsh and Germans, then Irish and Eastern Europeans. The village is off Route 940. Follow signs to the site, which is open Monday through Saturday, 9:00 A.M. to 5:00 P.M.; noon to 5:00 P.M. on Sunday. It is closed holidays except Memorial Day, July 4, and Labor Day. Admission fee is $3.50. For more information write to the Village at R.R. 2, Box 236, Weatherly 18255, or call (570) 636–2070.

Another coal locale is the *Pioneer Tunnel Coal Mine* in Ashland. The mine, a nonprofit community project, was blasted shut as a commercial operation in 1931 and opened to the public in 1962. It is a drift mine that tunnels almost horizontally 1/2-mile into Mahanoy Mountain. The tunnel follows an anthracite vein that is nearly 200 feet thick in some places (200 feet is huge, mine-wise). In many mines, veins were so small that men had to lie down to work, but in Pioneer miners could work standing up. You may take a half-hour tour ($6.00 per adult) in an open coal car pulled by a battery-powered mine motor; the tour begins at the entrance of the mine, journeying 1,800 feet into Mahanoy Mountain, then passes the big vein, where visible tunnels branch off. The other half-hour train tour ($4.00 per adult) goes around the outside of the mountain, not through tunnels. A steam locomotive, called a *lokie*, pulls the train past an open pit mine that was dug close to the surface with steam shovels and a "bootleg hole" where poachers dug out coal.

To get to the Pioneer Mine, take Route 61 into Ashland, where it becomes Center Street. Turn left (south) on Twentieth Street and continue for 3 blocks. The mine is open from Memorial Day to Labor Day, 10:00 A.M. to 6:00 P.M. daily. Call (570) 875–3850 for hours in April, May, September, and October; closed the rest of the year.

Walk across Higher-Ups Park to the *Anthracite Museum*, featuring a collection of tools, machinery, and photographs showing how anthracite, or hard coal, has been mined from the early pick-and-shovel days to contemporary surface-mining operations. The museum is open from April 1 through November 30, 10:00 A.M. to 6:00 P.M. Monday through Saturday; noon to 6:00 P.M. Sunday. Closed the rest of the year. Admission is $3.50. For more information call (570) 875–4708, or write to the museum at Pine and Seventeenth Streets, Ashland 17921.

Check out Nesquahoning, a mining town on Route 209, southeast of Hazleton. Nesquahoning is built on hills so steep that nothing seems level. Driving slowly, you can peek through a barbershop window to glimpse an elderly gentleman getting a haircut. In front of the homes, flowers spill from their beds over cement walls toward the sidewalk. In backyards, women hang laundry to dry on clotheslines. Then you're through town, and signs usher you down the mountain into Jim Thorpe.

Little Switzerland

Until about 1950, Mauch Chunk was another Pennsylvania mining town whose economy fluctuated with the coal market, where miners lived in uncertainty and millionaires lived in mansions. Trying to survive, citizens of Mauch (rhymes with *hawk*) Chunk and East Mauch Chunk donated a nickel a week to an economic development fund. In 1954 the towns merged and became Jim Thorpe. If you love small towns, you'll love Jim Thorpe.

Mauch Chunk's history is synonymous with coal mining and railway transport. Josiah White, a self-taught civil engineer and founder of the Lehigh Coal & Navigation Company, designed and invented a device to schlep his coal to his canal. He contrived the switchback railroad, which followed the Delaware Canal to Philadelphia or the Morris Canal to New York City, and which jokers refer to as the first roller coaster. The 9-mile Gravity Road was completed in 1827; ten wagons, each carrying 1.5 tons of coal, traveled down Summit Hill powered entirely by gravity. Mules pulled the empty cars up the incline, then got a free ride down. After the demand for coal diminished, the train was used by tourists.

Driving down the highway into the heart of Jim Thorpe, you quickly realize why locals call their home Little Switzerland. (Little Colorado

"Thanks, King"

Controversy in the Olympics didn't start with murder in Munich or bribery in Salt Lake City. In 1912 in Stockholm, Sweden, Jim Thorpe, a Native American from Oklahoma, won gold medals in the pentathlon and decathlon. King Gustav V, presenting the medals to the twenty-four-year-old, said, "You, Sir, are the greatest athlete in the world." To which Thorpe replied, "Thanks, King." When the International Olympic Committee (IOC) learned that Thorpe had earlier played semipro baseball, earning $2.00 a game, it demanded that he return his trophies, which he did. He later played baseball for the New York Giants, Cincinnati Reds, and Boston Braves and football for the New York Giants and other teams. After retiring from professional sports, Thorpe played bit parts in several Hollywood movies. When he died of cancer, penniless, in 1953, Oklahoma refused to build him a monument, so his widow started looking for a place where her husband and hero could be buried with honor. She found Mauch Chunk and East Mauch Chunk, which voted to consolidate their communities as Jim Thorpe Borough. In 1982 the IOC reinstated Thorpe's amateur status and gave his family replicas of his gold medals. Thorpe's grave is on Route 903.

would have worked, too.) Park in a public lot (or at a meter, where a quarter still buys an hour) to explore the narrow, winding streets on foot. This area at the foot of the hills is Hazard Square. It quickly becomes obvious how it got its name. Drive and walk defensively, please.

Of the twenty-six million-aires living in the United States before World War II, thirteen had homes in Mauch Chunk.

On the square, in the Jim Thorpe Railroad Station, you can buy tickets for rides on steam locomotive trains through the mountains to Nesqua-honing, an 8-mile round trip, in spring and summer. During the autumn foliage season, trips of nearly three hours to Haucks and back leave twice a day. Tickets for the short trip are under $5.00, for the longer trip about $12.00. For complete schedules and rates, write Rail Tours, Inc., P.O. Box 285, Jim Thorpe 18229, or call (570) 325–4606.

Across the square from the station, you see the **Hooven Mercantile Company**. On the first floor, specialty shops laid out in emporium fashion, without partitions, feature coal jewelry, dolls, decorated eggs, and various other craft items and supplies. Upstairs is the **Old Mauch Chunk Scale Model Railroad HO Display,** a train-lover's exposition with thirteen model trains that pull cars over more than a thousand feet of track. Hours vary seasonally, so it's a good idea to call ahead (570–325–2248). Modest admission fee.

Drive up the hill on US Route 209 to tour the **Asa Packer Mansion**, providing a dramatic contrast to the cabins of Eckley Miner's Village at Hazleton. Asa Packer is said to have worked his way from humble beginnings to become the founder and president of Lehigh Valley Railroad, founder of Lehigh University, and a philanthropist on a grand scale. In 1860 European craftsmen built the Victorian home,

Molly Who?

*I*n the late 1870s a group of men were hanged in the Mauch Chunk Jail (now the Old Jail Museum in Jim Thorpe) for murdering two mine bosses. The men were members of a group called the Molly Maguires, Irish immigrants who fled the famine and found a dismal existence in the mines of Northeastern Pennsylvania. Poor pay and rotten working conditions led to a strike, which led to management hiring a spy, which led to long-term controversy. Before the trial, which the coal companies financed, all newspaper reports called the men killers. See Sean Connery and Richard Harris in the movie The Molly Maguires, and decide for yourself the guilt or innocence of the executed men.

lavishly decorated and furnished in mid-nineteenth–century opulence. It stands today as it did when the Packers celebrated their fiftieth wedding anniversary, preserved rather than restored. Among the outstanding pieces are the first-prize gas chandelier of the 1876 Centennial Exposition in Philadelphia. Producers of the film *Gone with the Wind* wanted to use the chandelier. "Frankly, my dear, no way," was the response, so the movie moguls made a perfect copy. You'll find collections of carved walnut furniture, paintings, sculpture, crystal, and china. Hours of operation are 11:00 A.M. to 4:15 P.M. daily, June through October; weekends only, April, May, and November. Modest admission fee. Write to P.O. Box 108, Jim Thorpe 18229, or call (570) 325–3229 for more details.

Trivia

In Mauch Chunk, now Jim Thorpe, miners in 1913 earned twenty-three cents an hour.

Asa gave his son, Harry, the brick-and-stone Second Empire–style mansion next door as a wedding gift. This house is lavish, too, with hand-decorated ceilings and Victorian antiques, including some pieces that belonged to the Packer family. The **Harry Packer Mansion** (Packer Hill), open for tours Sunday from noon to 4:00 P.M., operates as a bed-and-breakfast inn, with thirteen rooms. The mansion has mystery weekends and sometimes turns over the entire establishment to wedding parties and special celebrations, so be sure to call ahead. Write P.O. Box 458, Jim Thorpe 18229, or phone (570) 325–8566.

One block south of Broadway, Race Street, a narrow alley, winds along the path once taken by an old mill race and passes old buildings, more specialty shops, and the stretch of stone facades called Stone Row, built by Asa Packer in 1848. Today longtime residents and shopkeepers live side by side with newly arrived artists and writers.

Don't miss **St. Mark's Episcopal Church** at 21 Race Street. The church is considered one of the most notable of the late Gothic Revival churches in Pennsylvania. It was built in 1869 by Richard Upjohn, the architect who was responsible for the Third Trinity Church of New York City. St. Mark's in Jim Thorpe is laid out in the form of a Latin cross, with an altar of white Italian marble, Minton tile floors, and Tiffany windows. The reredos (which is the stone behind the altar), made of Caen stone, is a memorial to Asa Packer. Half-hour tours are held daily, June through October, at 1:15, 2:00, 2:45, and 3:30 P.M. Call (570) 325–2241 for more information.

While Jim Thorpe is an historian's heaven, it's also a sportsperson's bliss. Hiking and biking trails attract athletes from hundreds of miles away. Of the several outfitters in Jim Thorpe, you can't do better than **Blue Mountain Sports** (just off Hazard Square at 34 Susquehanna Street). Of course owners Tom and Elissa Marsden sell clothes and equipment, but they do more: They know and love the area, and they talk, as long as you wish, about the best paths and routes for your particular preferences. Visit their Web site at www.bikejimthorpe.com, or call at (570) 325–4421 or (800) 599–4421.

For more information about the town, call the tourist center toll-free at (888) 546–8467.

Just outside of Jim Thorpe, overlooking Route 209 at the base of Mount Pisgah is a memorial plaque on a large rock where the village of Northern Liberties used to be. In 1861 virtually all the village males between the ages of sixteen and twenty-six volunteered to serve the Union in the Civil War; their wholesale death effectively destroyed the village by killing off its reproductive population. All that remains is the plaque memorializing the soldiers.

Consider **Country Junction** a transition from the old world into the new. Country Junction may or may not be the world's largest general store, as it claims, but once you sing a few tunes with the life-size statues of the Blues Brothers and have a conversation with the parrot, you won't care. It's a hoot, this rural version of a shopping mall. Buy a wall plaque that says, I FISH, THEREFORE I LIE. Pick up potted plants, plaid pillows, or purple paint. Look at lawn ornaments, lumber, and light bulbs. Country Junction is open seven days a week; Route 209, 4 miles west of I–476. Call (570) 377–5050.

The Poconos

The Pocono Mountains, northern foothills of the Appalachian range, are diminutive when compared with the Rockies—but they're right here, within easy reach of the Boston-to-Washington (Bo-Wash) corridor and its multitudes. The highest Pocono—the impressively named Mount Ararat, in Preston, Wayne County—towers 2,654 feet above sea level. Not high enough to give you altitude sickness, it can, however, promote a natural high, if you love getting away from the madding crowds. Best known for honeymoon hideaways, the Poconos also offer welcome respite from flatland woes. City dwellers, mostly from Pennsylvania, New Jersey, and New York, find that looking up at the tall evergreen and deciduous trees, looking out over serene ponds and lakes, looking inward with pleasure, brings immense peace and

Sure, You Can Rent a Horse for a Ride

Y ou can also rent a mule, if the folks back home aren't stubborn enough. Call (570) 839–6333 to reach the Pocono Adventures Riding Stable, a mile south of Mt. Pocono, off Route 611 on Meadowside Road.

relaxation. Even those who jokingly call the Poconos "the Pinocchios" aren't lying when they say how much they enjoy the local mountains.

To see some of the lesser known parts of the Poconos, take Route 209 out of Jim Thorpe toward Lehighton. In its time, Route 209 was a major highway, important enough for its construction to displace homes and cemeteries and prize stands of sugar maples. This route has lost much tourist traffic to interstates; here and there you still see a failed group of tourist cabins predating today's motels or an abandoned gas station with weeds growing through the macadam. These properties might be good investments for people who can afford to wait for a return, because I–80 often resembles a parking area for trucks hauling double trailers up the mountains. One can imagine traffic returning to Route 209 in sheer desperation. By today's standards it's narrow and slow because of the steep hills and curves, but the surface is in fairly good condition, trucks pull over to let traffic pass, and most of the country-side is lovely. Even where it's not beautiful, it's interesting. This highway skirts Lehighton.

In Lehighton most folks speak in Pennsylvania Dutch accents; many have lived here all their lives, as have their parents, grandparents, and even great-grandparents.

Continue north on Route 209, then turn right, south, on Old Route 115. Turn left on Lower Cherry Valley Road, and follow the signs into the **Cherry Valley Vineyards**, a friendly little winery run by the Sorrenti family. (From Route 33, take the Saylorsburg exit, then Old Route 115 south, and follow signs.) The Sorrentis produce a limited amount of Chardonnay that they say has a "dry, delicate, incredibly wonderful balance" plus a dry champagne and several fruity, semidry wines. The winery is open seven days a week, 11:00 A.M. to 5:00 P.M., for tastings and sales. Tours, which include information about the wine's fermentation, filtering, and bottling processes, are led weekends, from 1:00 to 5:00 P.M., March through December. For more information you can write to the vineyard at RR 5, Box 5100, Saylorsburg 18353; call (570) 992–2255, or visit www.cherryvalleyvineyard.com.

A quick jog back on Route 33 north takes you to Snydersville, which isn't much more than a gas station, a school bus stop, and antiques dealers in old homes. The names and proprietors may change, but this remains a good area for antiquing, where the dealers are knowledgeable but not in the thick of the tourist stream.

At Snydersville, pick up Business Route 209 (paralleling the four-lane Route 209) going south. Turn right on Hickory Valley Road and follow the signs to *Quiet Valley Living Historical Farm*. (If you start in Stroudsburg, take Business Route 209 north, left on Hickory Valley Road, and follow signs.) Alice and Wendell Wicks, with their daughter and son-in-law, Sue and Gary Oiler, saw the possibilities for this centuries-old Pennsylvania German farm. The Wicks and the Oilers have invested work, time, and money in researching, repairing, and collecting furnishings and farm equipment. In 1963 they opened Quiet Valley as a living museum, showing how the original Pennsylvania Dutch family lived on this virtually self-sufficient homestead from about 1770 to 1913. The families restored the existing buildings to full function and reconstructed others that would have been there; for a while the Oilers lived in the top floor of the home. "We don't own it any more," says Sue Oiler. "It's now a private, nonprofit organization. My home is in the middle of a nonprofit farm. In my head I know it's not really mine, but in my heart I care for it and love it as if it were."

Using costumed area residents as role players, Quiet Valley takes you through the daily routines and seasonal activities of the colonial family. One of the most interesting parts of the tour is the earthen-floored cellar kitchen in the main building. At first the settling family lived entirely in this room, with only the clay-hearth fireplace for heat and cooking. A

Baby, It's Cold Outside #1

*S*o why not try ice-fishing in the Poconos? State-owned lakes with easy public access and big, hungry fish include Tobyhanna Lake, Lake Wallenpaupack, Promised Land Lake, Beltzville Dam, and Pecks Pond. Occasionally Kettle Creek Wildlife Sanctuary, in the Monroe County Environmental Education Center near Bartonsville, runs an ice-fishing clinic.

(That's to learn how to ice-fish, not to recuperate from the ensuing chill.) Call (570) 629–3061. Old joke: How do you catch a fish in the winter? Gather a hammer, a can of peas, and a can opener. Dig a hole in the ice. Using the can opener, open the can of peas. Place the peas around the edge of the hole. As each fish comes up to take a pea, hit it on the head with a hammer.

costumed guide uses the cooking utensils and talks about her "life" as a colonial woman. Outside, your kids can pet the animals and jump in the hay, even if they end up a little dirty and itchy. After the tour, consider picnicking in the grove. Quiet Valley is open Tuesday through Saturday, June 20 to Labor Day, 10:00 A.M. to 5:30 P.M. weekdays and 1:00 to 5:30 P.M. Sunday. The last tour begins at 4:00 P.M. Cost is $7.00 per adult. For more information write to Quiet Valley Living Historical Farm, 1000 Turkey Hill Road, Stroudsburg 18360. E-mail the museum/farm at qvfarm@ptolprolog.net, or call (570) 992–6161.

The Poconos offer options for every imaginable enthusiasm—as well as some unimaginable ones. For most of us, auto racing is a spectator sport. But the 2¹/₂-mile race course *Pocono Raceway* holds the *Roos Racing School*. Go equipped with a driver's license, sneakers, gloves, and experience handling a standard shift. The raceway provides instruction, race cars, racetracks, colorful driving suits, and helmets. Your instructor will show you where to brake, when to accelerate, how to handle corners, and, presumably, how to pray for safety. Call Roos at (800) 722–3669. The office is on Route 115 in Blakeslee.

Consider popping into the *Pocono Cheesecake Factory* (Route 611, Swiftwater), where chefs prepare up to a hundred cheesecakes daily. Watch through the giant window as almonds, raspberries, chocolate chips, and liqueurs blend into the dessert of your choice. A drooling visitor recently estimated that she could count 700 springform pans, and

Baby, It's Cold Outside #2

*W*hy not try snow tubing in the Poconos? If you wish to swish downhill without standing up, if you always loved sledding except for towing the sled back uphill, this is the sport for you. Six ski areas offer snow tubing parks during ski season, off the beaten ski trail. All except Jack Frost are lighted for evening tubing.

- **Camelback Ski Area,** *Tannersville; (570) 629–1661, extension 123.*

- **Alpine Mountain,** *Analomink; (570) 595–2150.*

- **Big Boulder Ski Area,** *Lake Harmony; (570) 772–0110 or (800) 468–2442.*

- **Blue Mountain Ski Area,** *Palmerton; (610) 826–7700.*

- **Jack Frost Mountain,** *White Haven (near Blakeslee); (570) 443–8425 or (800) 468–2442.*

- **Shawnee Mountain,** *Shawnee-on-Delaware; (570) 421–7231.*

she worried who was going to clean them. As you choose between your wallet and your waistline, read the sign: LIFE IS UNCERTAIN. EAT DESSERT FIRST. Call (570) 839–6844 for prices, hours, and calorie counts.

A few doors away, also on Route 611 in Swiftwater, drop into *Skip's Western Wear* to touch and test crinolines, saddles, and square-dancing shirts—in case you need them. Phone (570) 839–8002; fax (570) 838–8034.

Heading north on 611, turn east in Mount Pocono on Route 940, then north on Route 191. Every roll of the tires takes you farther away from civilization. Stop in Mountainhome to visit the *Theo B. Price Lumber Company*, a singular hardware-and-quilts store with a distinctly downhome—okay, Mountainhome—flavor. On the street level, with its uneven wooden plank flooring, amidst the nails and feed, you can find solutions for problems you didn't know you had—until you see the solutions. Upstairs are hand-sewn and handcrafted goods for the home, the friends, and the soul. Shopkeeper Maryann Miller manages the emporium started in 1908 by her grandfather, Theo, who invented tools and devices for mines. His original cash register, capable of ringing sales as high as twenty dollars, sits in the back of the place. Hours are 8:00 A.M. to 5:00 P.M., except Sunday. Call (570) 595–2501.

Eight miles up Route 191, in beautiful downtown LaAnna—wait, you missed downtown, those were two deer, not two diners or two dress shops—you can visit *Holley Ross Pottery*. Daily from 9:30 A.M. to 5:30 P.M. and Sunday from 1:00 to 5:30 P.M., you can watch pottery being made and buy a variety of glass and ceramic items. The pottery is closed December through April. Call (570) 676–3248.

Speaking of destruction . . . It's not entirely clear what personality type

From Tanneries to Tannersville

*W*hether or not you stop in Tannersville, you'll certainly drive through it. While you're waiting for the traffic light to change, know this: Early on, the Lenni Lenape Indians lived in this valley in the foothills of the Poconos. In about 1750 John Larned bought the land and built a log tavern and two grist mills. Twenty-nine years later,

General Sullivan and his army, en route to the Wyoming Valley, spent the night in tents next to the tavern. In 1834 Jacob Singmaster built a large tannery, which became the village's main industry and inspired the name change from Larneds to Tannersville. Fire destroyed several tanneries, but innumerable candle shops keep the heat on.

likes paintball, but if you like murder and mayhem, if you love war, paintball is for you. And paintball is everywhere in the Poconos. This competitive outdoor "sport" involves balls of water-soluble, biodegradable, nontoxic paint, which you shoot at your friends or enemies. Ride a military troop transport to a mountaintop with a beautiful view—in order to shoot paint. Your $20- to $30-per-person all-day pass entitles you to fifty paintballs, all-you-can-use carbon dioxide as a propellant, and protective head gear and face mask. You can rent a camouflage suit, which might be a good idea, since the games are called "attack and defend," "hostile takeover," and "total elimination." Call ahead to reserve a field at **Skirmish** (Route 903, Jim Thorpe; 800–745–7647 or 570–325–3654). There's also **Splatter Paintball Games,** at Jack Frost Mountain (Route 940, Blakeslee 800–468–2442).

For the back-to-nature gang—and even for people who prefer their nature in *National Geographic* specials—**Hickory Run State Park**, especially the **Boulder Field**, is not to be believed and never to be forgotten. This area, now a National Natural Landmark (say that fast three times) has remained essentially unchanged for 20,000 years, give or take. Boulders up to 26 feet long cover an area 400 feet by 1,800 feet, and you're welcome to climb, scramble, or sit on them—if you can. Imagine a dish of one-inch pebbles, and imagine an ant trying to navigate the terrain. The ground beneath the boulders is totally flat and free of vegetation. Staggering.

Of course, like any self-respecting state park, Hickory Run has trails, campgrounds, and picnic facilities. You may apply for hunting and fishing licenses and try your luck in the park's 15,500 acres. You may swim in summer and snowmobile, cross-country ski, and sled in winter. But what should lure you miles out of your way—and what will indubitably entice you back—is the Boulder Field. Hickory Run is immediately southeast of the intersection of I–476 and I–80, so it's hard to miss if you're in the area. You can write to the park office at Box 81, White Haven 18661; or call (570) 443–0400.

Perhaps you'd like to find the bluebird of happiness while you're in the Poconos? No problem. Take the 53-mile auto tour, with twelve stops and six suggested side trips, that follows John James Audubon's 1829 journey into the forests of the Lehigh River Valley. John James Audubon is the famed nineteenth-century naturalist who traveled, observed, painted, and wrote about birds and other wildlife. He lived in Pennsylvania and traveled extensively throughout Pennsylvania and the United States. The aim of Audubon's America Program is to help conserve, restore, enhance, interpret, and protect natural and cultural resources.

From Hickory Run State Park, turn east on Route 534 to Albrightsville; south on Route 903 to Jim Thorpe; west on Route 209, and north on Route 93 to Hudsondale; north on Hudsondale Drive, through Rockport; then back to Hickory Run on 534. Or, for kicks, travel counterclockwise. You may drive the circuit with "Pennsylvania Polka" on the radio or buy an audiocassette tour from Greater Wyoming Valley Audubon Society, P.O. Box 535, Dallas 18612; or call (570) 825–2473. For cassette and phone orders, call (888) 546–8467 weekdays, 9:00 A.M. to 4:00 P.M. and weekends, 10:00 A.M. to 5:00 P.M. The Web site is www.webstreetmall.com/audubon. You can also buy the $14.95 tapes at the Jim Thorpe Train Station.

Delaware Water Gap

*H*ere you are close to the ***Delaware Water Gap National Recreation Area,*** which runs along a 40-mile stretch of the Delaware River in New Jersey and Pennsylvania. Publicity calls it "the eighth wonder of the world." The town of Delaware Water Gap marks the southernmost point of the 70,000-acre recreation area, which became federal property in 1965. At the **Bushkill Visitor Center** (Route 209 in Bushkill), you'll find park information and a bookstore. Since hours vary seasonally, you might want to visit www.nps.gov/dewa or call ahead (570) 588–7044.

Even in the nineteenth century this gap attracted the well-to-do for resort holidays away from the heat. Horse-drawn carriages and rafts transported early visitors until about 1856, when the Delaware and Cobb's Gap Railroad Company opened a track to Scranton. Native Americans called the area Pohoqauline, Pahaqalong, and Pahaqualia (pronunciations are optional), all of which mean "river passing between two mountains." Its beauty lies partly in the contrasting colors of layers of quartzite, red sandstone, and dark shale that have been revealed as the river carved its path over geologic eons.

With light hiking, you can appreciate the gap close at hand. Park in the Resort Point parking lot off Route 611, on the Pennsylvania side. Across the road, stone steps take you to a trail paralleling a stream that goes up steeply for a short distance, then turns left onto a marked trail. The trail continues gently upward for about a mile; when you get to a waterfall, you can no longer hear the highway traffic. A little farther straight ahead, a large rock outcropping overlooks the entire gap and steals your breath. It's picture-postcard pretty. In this area you can also drive into some well-marked overlook points from which you see a spectacular

Delaware Water Gap

view without hiking. At one such place a souped-up red Chevrolet once roared in; a couple of teenagers slurping diet Cokes looked out, said, "There isn't anything here," and roared away. Pushing these types of people over the edge is against park regulations. For full information on the Delaware Water Gap National Recreation Area, write to the offices, Bushkill 18324, or call (570) 588–2451.

One way to see some of this without driving is to ride the *Delaware Water Gap Trolley*. Guides explain the history, points of interest, settlers, and Indians, and the entire natural splendor of the gap. The trolley operates from late March through November, and the depot is on Route 611 at the center of Delaware Water Gap. Call (570) 476–9766 or (570) 476–6473.

In the same area, off Route 209 at Bushkill, the *Mary Stolz Doll Museum* features about 125 dolls representing cultures from around the world, plus old toys and miniature rooms. Mary started collecting dolls in 1910, and Bill and Jan Stolz, the fourth generation, continue to operate the museum. While looking without touching isn't difficult, looking without owning can be torture for a committed collector. The gift shop offers boundless collection possibilities: dolls, teddy bears, dollhouses, and trains. The museum is open seven days a week, except in slow seasons, when it closes Monday; for more information call (570) 588–7566.

Directly across from the doll museum, the **Pocono Indian Museum** shows the history of the now-extinct Delaware Indians in six rooms of collected artifacts. Some pottery is more than 1,000 years old, and weapons and tools have had only their handles reconstructed. As you look at the exhibits, you can listen to a half-hour cassette explaining the displays. The Delaware Indians wore simple deerskin garments, cut their hair short, and wore no feathers, except perhaps for ceremonies. Nor did they live in tepees. The museum holds a reconstructed house of the kind the Delawares made by lashing together saplings and covering them with strips of elm or oak bark. Another room exhibits artifacts from various western Indian tribes, even a 150-year-old scalp. If that seems a little gory, you can cover your eyes as you pass. Museum and gift shop hours are open daily, 9:00 A.M. to 7:00 P.M. in the summer; 9:30 A.M. to 5:30 P.M. beginning in September. Admission costs $4.00 for adults. For more information write to the museum at P.O. Box 261, Bushkill 18324. E-mail them at dream38@ptd.net or call (570) 588–9338.

Also on Route 209 at Bushkill, the **Pennsylvania Crafts Gallery** exhibits and sells the work of juried members of the Pennsylvania Guild of Craftsmen: weaving, pottery, precious and nonprecious metals, leather, basketry, and such. Its opening hours vary, so call (570) 588–9156 to check.

Even more glorious than the creations of any human hand, **Bushkill Falls**, called the Niagara of Pennsylvania, is easy to reach, 2 miles northwest of US Route 209. Easy walking over rustic bridges and a nature trail of about 1¹/₂ miles takes you through virgin forests, past a gorge with a view of eight waterfalls, the largest of which is Bushkill, dropping 100 feet. Even with a simple camera it's possible to take spectacular pictures. You may picnic, boat, and fish in the park. Some food is available. The park is open daily, 9:00 A.M. to dusk, April through November. Rates are moderate. Call (570) 588–6682.

At Dingmans Ferry, farther north on Route 209 but still in the Delaware Water Gap National Recreational Area, **Dingmans Falls,** the highest waterfall in Pennsylvania, pours down over 100 feet of rock with awesome power. On the same easy trail, in woods of hemlock and ferns, **Silver Thread Falls,** not quite as high but equally beautiful, is another stop worth a few photographs. In the park's nature center, you can study an audiovisual program or pick up a map and talk to a naturalist about the falls and good trails—including easy ones—to walk.

From Dingmans Ferry it's only about 10 miles to Milford, a good place to spend the night—or several nights if you can spare the time. A good choice is the **Cliff Park Inn,** completely surrounded by a golf course that has been in operation since 1913. Talk about a mature course! This inn, an 1820 farmhouse, has two dining rooms serving food one guest called "a gourmet's dream." She was hooked by the quail stuffed with raisins and apples, flamed in brandy, and covered with a truffle sauce. Since the menu changes periodically, you may find not quail but some other exotic offering, such as a game pie or beef Wellington. In winter, when even the fanatics don't golf in Pennsylvania, the golf course is used for cross-country skiing. So are the nearby hiking trails. The inn has 570 acres of woods and a view that overlooks three states. You can rent golf or cross-country equipment at the inn, owned for five generations by the Buchanan family. Call ahead (570–296–6491 or 800–225–6535) to reserve one of the eighteen rooms, each with private bath. E-mail cpi@warwick.net, surf at www.cliffparkinn.com, or write to the inn at Milford 18337.

In Milford stop at the **Upper Mill**, a nineteenth-century mill where water rushing over a three-story-high waterwheel used to power a grindstone. The mill building, on the National Register of Historic Places, is open year-round with an easy-to-follow self-guided tour, and the waterwheel operates from May to Thanksgiving, 9:00 A.M. to 5:00 P.M. daily. The only power generated in the mill these days is retail power, but that, fortunately, is thriving. From the cafe and bar, you can watch the waterwheel. While you're there you'll also want to visit the bakery, gift shop, bookstore, and dress boutique. The mill (570–296–5141) is on Sawkill Creek and Water and Mill Streets.

From Milford, driving west on I–84 for about half an hour brings you to the **Sterling Inn**, in South Sterling. It has sixty-six rooms, a third with fireplaces or Franklin stoves. The inn sits on more than a hundred acres, with hiking and cross-country ski trails, a tennis court, and a swimming and skating pond. Call the cuisine traditional American country gourmet, and expect beef, chicken, and seafood. Since this is the health-food age, the inn presents vegetarian options, too. Saturday-night entertainment is live jazz or contemporary music. For rates and reservations e-mail thesterlinginn@ezaccess.net, find it on the Internet at www.thesterlinginn.com, write Sterling Inn, Route 191, South Sterling 18460, or call (570) 676–3311 or (800) 523–8200.

For a different kind of stay, go northwest from Milford on Route 6 to the *Settler's Inn*, a twenty-room country lodge furnished in antiques and white wicker. The inn is run by Grant and Jeanne Genzlinger with help from family and friends. The menu, which features local produce and local trout and pheasant, changes every four months—"except for the smoked-trout appetizer, which we can't take off the menu," says Jeanne. The inn is near Lake Wallenpaupack, where you can fish and boat. For more information about Settler's Inn, write 4 Main Avenue, Hawley 18428; call (570) 226–2993 or (800) 833–8527. E-mail the inn at settler@ptd.net, or check out www.thesettlersinn.com.

Upper Delaware Wilds

The Lackawaxen area remains unspoiled. Although the land along the Delaware River and the Lackawaxen River is privately owned, the stretch of the Delaware from Port Jervis to Hancock (both towns in New York State) is protected under the Wild and Scenic Rivers Act. You'll find most of the historic and natural attractions along or near Route 590. The village of Lackawaxen (Indian word for "swift waters") is named for the river that flows into the Delaware. If you're a fishing enthusiast, you'll like the Lackawaxen Fishing and Boat Access, operated by the Pennsylvania Fish and Boat Commission, which provides good fishing where the Delaware River runs deep and slow.

Across from the fishing access is the *Zane Grey Museum*, representing a classic American success story. Zane Grey was a dentist. He attended the University of Pennsylvania, where he received his degree in 1896. "He played on the Penn varsity baseball team and was quite well known," says Dot Moon, curator at the museum. "Baseball was very different than it is today. College baseball was a very big thing." After college Zane Grey played baseball for the Orange Athletic Club in the Eastern League, which was considered a "gentlemen's league." Moon says that means they played for money but did not play on Sunday as "professional" baseball players did. In the off season, Grey practiced dentistry.

> **Trivia**
>
> *Lake Wallenpaupack, an artificial lake north of Route 84, east of Route 191, covered old farm lands. Divers can still see stone walls, marking the perimeters of some farmers' pastures.*

Grey's first article, a fishing story, was published in 1902. He gave up baseball after the 1902 season at the urging of his future wife, who encouraged him to devote himself to writing. In 1903 he wrote his first novel, *Betty Zane*, the story of his great-great aunt who helped save Fort

Trivia

A popular horse race that was 5 miles long used to take place between Camptown and Wyalusing. The race is believed to have inspired Stephen Foster, who was visiting his brother in Towanda, to write "Camptown Races." Doo-da, doo-da.

Henry during the Revolutionary War. He moved to Lackawaxen in 1905 to devote himself to writing and later said the Lackawaxen area was where he first became familiar with "really wild country." Between 1902 and 1909 Gray wrote articles for popular magazines on fishing and adventure, and in 1908 he wrote about his adventures in the Grand Canyon. While he was on this western trip, he began writing his first novel about the West, *Heritage of the Desert.*

After leaving Lackawaxen, Zane Grey traveled extensively to exotic places, such as Tahiti and New Zealand, to research his books. They were so convincing that Hollywood took to them, and by 1918 Grey left for California to work with the people producing movies based on his books. His Lackawaxen home remains as a museum containing mementos of his life. Grey and his wife are buried in the cemetery of St. Mark's Lutheran Church (built in 1848) along with the body of an unknown soldier killed during the Battle of Minisink in 1779, during the Revolutionary War. For more details call the National Park Service, Upper Delaware Council, at (914) 252–3022.

From the fishing access you can also see **Roebling's Delaware Aqueduct**, the oldest suspension bridge in use today. John Roebling (who designed the Brooklyn Bridge but died before it was built and also created the Three Sisters bridges in Pittsburgh), designed and built four aqueducts for the Delaware and Hudson (D&H) Canal; only this one remains. Completed in 1849, the aqueduct connected the canal between Lackawaxen, in Pennsylvania, and New York. The aqueduct fell into disrepair and was later restored by the National Park Service. Now it is sturdy enough to be used, a century and a half later, as an automobile thoroughfare. (Locals—and local signs—call it the **Roebling Bridge**.)

A nice place to stay, where owner JoAnn Jahn is deeply engrossed in local history, is the **Roebling Inn** on the Delaware. It's on Scenic Drive off Route 590 at Lackawaxen. Jahn says the white clapboard inn with green shutters and roof was built in about 1870 and was used as an office for the D&H Canal company. The six guest rooms, decorated with country antiques, are modified for contemporary tastes with private baths, television, and queen-size beds; some rooms have fireplaces. From the inn you can walk to canoeing, golf, horseback riding, a bait shop, a lunch restaurant, a general store, whitewater rafting, tennis, river swimming, and a couple of great places for dinner. (Previous editions of this guide sent many visitors to the Roebling Inn because, says Jahn, "The title of the book says it all. We really are off the beaten path.") For full details and reservations, write P.O. Box 31, Lackawaxen 18435, or call (570) 685–7900. E-mail JoAnn at roebling@ltis.net, or find her at www.poconos. org/ members/roeblinginn.

You can find considerably more rustic accommodations at *Sylvania Tree Farm* on the Delaware River in Mast Hope. It's a tree farm—a naturalist's paradise—where you can stay in a modern cottage or pitch your tent at a campsite. Mast Hope is one of those you-can't-get-there-from-here places. From Milford take Route 6 about 14 miles; go north on Route 434 for 3 miles; take Route 590 west to Lackawaxen, then turn right toward Mast Hope. (Ask for a brochure with full directions when you make reservations.) The destination worth the trouble is 1,250 acres on the river shore with woods, fields, brooks, and seclusion. The property is in the Upper Delaware Wild and Scenic River corridor, administered by the National Park Service. Watchful visitors sight bald eagles and blue herons in the valley; and white-tailed deer, black bears, beavers, and foxes in the woods and fields. The fly-fishing crowd loves the farm's private stream. You can cross-country ski in winter, hike other times, and take canoe and rafting trips with nearby outfitters. In addition, the National Park Service gives tours of the river valley and several historic sites. Write Sylvania Tree Farm, 112 Mast Hope Road, Mast Hope, Lackawaxen 18435, or call (570) 685–7001. The e-mail address is mcksts@ltis. net, and the Web site is www.mckayenterprises.com.

Have a Medium Time in Scranton

For a while, Scranton was the thirty-seventh largest city in the United States; as such, it attracted traveling vaudeville acts. Well-known performers who played Scranton included Mae West, W. C. Fields, Will Rogers, Fred Astaire, the Marx Brothers, Fanny Brice, Buster Keaton, Ed Wynn, Jack Benny, George Burns and Gracie Allen, Ray Bolger, and, of course, Harry Houdini. According to the Houdini Museum, Scranton had a reputation as the toughest town on the show business circuit. Tough audiences probably included gruff immigrant foundry workers and coal miners. Performers used Scranton to try out new acts and to graduate from the "medium time" vaudeville circuit to the "big time." If the acts were well received, booking agents invited them to New York. Hence the saying evolved, "If you can make it in Scranton, you can make it anywhere!"

A Day Trip: Endless Mountains

Four adjoining counties—Bradford, Sullivan, Susquehanna, and Wyoming—form the Endless Mountains Heritage Region. More than 15,000 years ago, glaciers etched these stones, creating the North Branch of the Susquehanna River. Valleys that once held prehistoric agricultural settlements hold modern farms—plus white clapboard churches, basket shops, and quaint bed-and-breakfasts.

On a day trip from the Scranton area, you can reach almost to Versailles. At **French Azilum Historic Site**, somebody got the bright idea that the vista looked like *la belle France*. So, in 1793 they built a home-away-from home for Marie Antoinette. Unfortunately, the planned colony never happened, and Marie never got there. She lost her head. Keep your head—and keep your eyes on the road—as you drive north on Route 6, above Wyalusing, on the banks of the Susquehanna. The grounds are open May through October, Wednesday through Sunday, from 11:00 A.M. to 4:00 P.M. The house is also open for tours on those days during the peak months of June, July, and August. In May, September, and October, the house is open weekends only. Call (570) 265–3376 for more information.

From Wyalusing, take Route 706 north to Montrose where, by appointment, you can visit the **Center for Anti-Slavery Studies**. It's a start-up enterprise, and temporarily it's in **The Book Shop** at 2 South Main Street; telephone (570) 278–2273. Founder, manager, and general factotum of the center is Paul Gere, whose goal is to identify the sites of the Underground Railroad; to remodel Montrose's A.M.E. Church, which was a center for Abolitionist activity; and to praise significant figures, such as Jonathan Jasper Wright, in the war against slavery. Gere says Wright was the first African-American lawyer in Pennsylvania and the first African-American member of a state supreme court, a position he achieved in South Carolina in 1870.

For more information contact the **Endless Mountains Visitors Bureau**, 712 Route 6 East, Tunkhannock 18657; (800) 769–8999 or (570) 836–5431. Or visit www.endlessmountains.org or www.endlesstrails.org.

Easton

Color me beautiful and lime green. Color a tour of the *Crayola Factory*, where you can see how Crayola makes red, blue, and chartreuse crayons. Roll up your burnt sienna sleeves and enjoy the interactive projects and activities. Let your child—and the child in you—see things through rose-colored Magic Markers. Friends will be green with envy when you tell them you painted the museum pink. Get silly with Silly Putty. Have a perfectly periwinkle time. The factory and gift shop are at 18 Centre Square, Easton. For more information call (610) 515–8000 or (800) 272–9652. It's colorful—and noisy, with all the kids. Don't miss it.

For more information on Northeast Pennsylvania, call (800) 229–3526 or visit www.visitnepa.org.

Best Annual Events in Northeastern Pennsylvania

- One Saturday each January, you can go *turkey bowling* at Memorytown. Just roll the frozen bird toward the pins. On Grange Road, between routes 611 and 940, in Mount Pocono. Gobble (570) 839–1680.

- Sometime in January or February, depending on the weather, you can watch or participate in the *Sleigh Rally* on Route 87 in Forksville. Call (570) 946–4160.

- Last weekend in April, the *Endless Mountains Maple Festival* takes place in Alparon Park, Route 14, Troy. Call (570) 297–2971 for details.

- In May (usually the last two weekends) is the *Farm Animal Frolic,* a perfect time for wee people to touch wee animals. No tours, just hens and chicks, sheep and lambs, pigs and piglets—you get the picture. $3.00 per person. Quiet Valley Living Historical Farm (570–992–6161).

- There's a *Poetry Festival* every May. Call the Luzerne County tourism office at (888) 905–2872.

- Strike up the band. The Dorflinger Museum holds eight outdoor *summer concerts,* Saturday evenings at 6:00, from late June through mid-August (indoors in case of rain). Most tickets cost $15 per adult, and most adults think the money is well spent. For reservations call (570) 253–1185.

- One Sunday in June you can watch the *Pocono 500* NASCAR Race at the Pocono Raceway, one of NASCAR's most competitive tracks. Call the Luzerne County tourism office at (888) 905–2872, or call Pocono Raceway at (800) 722–3929.

- One Sunday in July you can watch the *Pennsylvania 500* NASCAR Race at Pocono Raceway. Call the Luzerne County tourism office at (888) 905–2872, or call Pocono Raceway at (800) 722–3929.

- From July 17 to 26 every year, you can attend a *novena at the Basilica of the Shrine of St. Ann* in Scranton. Call (570) 347–5691.

- Try the annual *Blueberry Festival,* first week in August, Montrose. For details call (570) 278–1881.

- In August Pittston holds a *Tomato Festival*. Call the Luzerne County tourism office at (888) 905–2872.
- Late August Towanda holds its *Riverfest* on River Street (of course). Call (570) 265–2696.
- For a lot of hot air, take in the *Shawnee Balloon Festival,* mid-October. Call (570) 421–7231.
- In autumn a *Harvest Festival* coincides with the weekend of Columbus Day. Since 1975 the festival has demonstrated how to make apple butter and keep bees, among other rural tricks. $5:00 per adult. Quiet Valley Living Historical Farm (570–992–6161).
- The first two weekends of December bring *Old Time Christmas,* with a live nativity, a bonfire, and participatory caroling. Count on a visit from Belschnikel, the folk character who visits Pennsylvania Dutch villages to see if children are good enough to earn holiday gifts. $5.00 per adult. Quiet Valley Living Historical Farm (570–992–6161).

PLACES TO STAY IN NORTHEASTERN PENNSYLVANIA

CANADENSIS
Overlook Inn, Dutch Hill Road; (570) 595–7519.

CLARKS SUMMIT
Inn at Nichols Village, 1101 Northern Boulevard; (570) 587–4124.

EAST STROUDSBURG
Inn at Meadowbrook, Cherry Lane Road; (570) 629–0296 or (800) 441–7619.

FRACKVILLE
Granny's Budget Host Inn, 115 West Coal Street; (570) 874–0408.

HAZLETON
Hazleton Motor Inn, 615 East Broad Street; (570) 459–1451.

JIM THORPE
Hotel Switzerland, 5 Hazard Square; (570) 325–4563. Ask about ski-and-stay and bike-and-stay packages.

Inn at Jim Thorpe, 24 Broadway; (800) 329–2599; www.innjt.com. Ask about ski-and-stay and bike-and-stay packages.

MOUNT POCONO
Farmhouse Bed & Breakfast, Box 6B; (570) 839–0796.

SCRANTON
Radisson Lackawanna Station Hotel, 700 Lackawanna Avenue; (570) 342–8300.

STROUDSBURG
Four Points Sheraton, 1220 West Main Street; (570) 424–1930; fax (570) 424–5909.

Plaza Hotel, 1220 West Main Street; (570) 424–1930 or (800) 777–5453.

WILKES-BARRE
Woodlands Inn & Resort, 1073 Route 315; (570) 824–9831.

PLACES TO EAT IN NORTHEASTERN PENNSYLVANIA

ASHLAND
Henry's Family Dining, Eleventh and Center Streets; (570) 875–1234.

Snyder's, 2114 Center Street; (570) 875–3320.

CLARKS SUMMIT
Ryah House at Inn at Nichols Village, 1101 Northern Boulevard; (570) 587–4124.

DELAWARE WATER GAP
Trail's End Café, Main Street; (570) 421–1928.

EAST STROUDSBURG
Dansbury Depot,
50 Crystal Street;
(570) 476–9480.

J R Green Scene, Interstate
80 at exit 51;
(570) 424–5451.

HAZLETON
Mike Dubatto's Library
Lounge Restaurant, 615
East Broad Street;
(570) 455–3920.

JIM THORPE
Emerald Restaurant and
Molly Maguires Pub at the
Inn at Jim Thorpe,
24 Broadway;
(800) 329–2599;
www.innjt.com.

JT's Steak & Ale House at
the Hotel Switzerland,
5 Hazard Square;
(570) 325–4563. Ask about
ski-and-stay and bike-and-
stay packages.

LAKE HARMONY
Blue Heron Grille, Lake
Shore Drive;
(570) 722–9898.

MARSHALLS CREEK
Big A, Route 209,
north of traffic light;
(570) 223–8314.

MILFORD
Dimmick Steak House, at
the traffic light;
(570) 296–4021.

MOUNTAINHOME
Mountainhome Diner,
Routes 191 and 390;
(570) 595–2523.

SCRANTON
Cooper's Seafood House &
Ship's Pub, Washington
Avenue and Pine Street;
(570) 346–6883

Tom & Jerry's Restaurant,
Pittston Avenue and Birch
Street; (570) 344–1771.

SHAWNEE-ON-DELAWARE
Saen, Shawnee Square;
(570) 476–4911.

SHOHOLA FALLS
Le Gorille (French for big,
hairy ape), Twin Lakes
Road; (570) 296–8094.

Stonehill, Route 6;
(570) 296–2624.

SNYDERSVILLE
Snydersville Diner,
Business Route 209;
(570) 992–4003.

STROUDSBURG
Mollie's, 622 Main Street;
(570) 476–4616.
Closed Tuesday.

TANNERSVILLE
Smuggler's Cove, Route
611; (570) 629–2277.

Appendix I

Pennsylvania Wineries

Adams County Winery, 251 Peach Tree Rd, Orrtanna 17353; phone (717) 334–4631; fax (717) 334–4026; adamscountywinery@blazenet.net.

Allegro Vineyards, RD 2, Box 64, Brogue 17309; phone (717) 927–9148.

Big Creek Vineyard, RR 5, Box 5270, Kunkletown 18058; phone (610) 681–3959; fax (610) 681–3960; bigcreek@ptdpostoffice.net.

Blue Mountain Vineyards, 7627 Grape Vine Drive, New Tripoli 18066; phone (610) 298–3068; fax (610) 298–8616; bmvsales@bmvc.com.

Brookmere Farm Vineyards, RD 1, Box 53, Route 655, Belleville 17004; phone (717) 935 5380; fax (717) 935–5349.

Buckingham Valley Vineyards, 1521 Route 413, Box 371, Buckingham 18912; phone (215) 794–7188; fax (215) 794–3606; gcforest@comcat.com pawine.com.

Calvaresi Winery, 107 Shartlesville Road, Bernville 19506; phone (610) 488–7966; fax (610) 488–1176.

Chaddsford Winery, 632 Baltimore Pike, Chadds Ford 19317; phone (610) 388–6221; fax (610) 388–0360; cfwine@chaddsford.com.

Cherry Valley Vineyard, Lower Cherry Valley Road RD 5, Box 5100 Saylorsburg 18353; phone (717) 992–2255; fax (717) 992 5083.

Christian W Klay Winery, P.O. Box 309, 412 Fayette Spring, Chalk Hill 15412; phone (724) 439–3424; fax (724) 439–1553; hhs.net/cwklay.

Clover Hill Vineyards & Winery, 9850 Newton Rd, Breinigsville 18031; phone (610) 395–2468; fax (610) 366–1246; clover01@fast.net.

Conneaut Cellars Winery, P.O. Box 5075, 12005 Conneaut Lake Road, Conneaut Lake 16316; phone (877) 229–9463; fax (814) 382–6151.

Country Creek Vineyard & Winery, 133 Cressman Road, Telford 18969; phone (215) 723–4348.

Evergreen Valley Vineyards, R.R. 1 Box 173-D, Evergreen Road, Luthersburg 15848; phone (814) 583–7575; fax (814) 583–7575.

Fox Ridge Vineyard & Winery, 3434 East Market Street, York 17402; phone (717) 755–3384; fax (717) 755–1248.

Franklin Hill Vineyards, 7833 Franklin Hill Road, Bangor 18013; phone (610) 588–8708; fax (610) 588–8158; vineyard@epix.net.

French Creek Ridge Vineyards, 200 Grove Road, Elverson 19520; phone (610) 286–7754; fax (610) 286–7772.

Galen Glen Vineyard, RD #1, Box 82-1, Winter Mountain Road, Andreas 18211; phone (717) 386–3682.

Glades Pike Winery, 2706 Glades Pike, Somerset 15501; phone (814) 445–3753; fax (814) 445–1856.

Heritage Wine Cellars, 12162 East Main Road, North East 16428; phone (800) 747–0083; fax (814) 725–8654.

Hunters Valley Winery, Box 326D, RD 2, Routes 11 & 15, Liverpool 17045; phone (717) 444–7211.

In & Out Vineyards, 258 Durham Road, Newtown 18940; phone (215) 860–5899; fax (215) 968–0941.

Lapic Winery, Ltd., 902 Tulip Drive, New Brighton 15066; phone (724) 846–2031; fax (724) 846–2031.

Laurel Mountain Vineyard, RD 1 Box 238, Falls Creek 15846; phone (814) 371–7022; fax (814) 371–7022; laurlmtn@penn.com wmcdata.com/laurel/.

Manatawny Creek Winery, 227 Levengood Road, Douglassville 19518; phone (610) 689–9804; fax (610) 689–9838.

Mazza Vineyards, 11815 East Lake Road, North East 16428-3363; phone (800) 796–9463; fax (814) 725–3948.

Mount Hope Estate & Winery, 83 Mansion House Road, Manheim 17545; phone (717) 665–7021; fax (717) 664–3466; royalspk@parenaissancefaire.com.

Mount Nittany Vineyard & Winery, RD 1, Box 138, Centre Hall 16828; phone (814) 466–6373; fax (814) 466–3066.

Naylor Wine Cellars, Inc., 4069 Vineyard Rd, Stewartstown 17363; phone (717) 993–2431; fax (717) 993–9460.

Nissley Vineyards, 140 Vintage Drive, Bainbridge 17502; phone (717) 426–3514; fax (717) 426–1391.

Oak Spring Winery, Route 220 North, RD 1 Box 612, Altoona 16602; phone (814) 946–3799; fax (814) 946–4245.

Oregon Hill Winery, 840 Oregon Hill, Morris 16938–9801; phone (717) 353–2711.

Peace Valley Winery, 300 Old Limekiln Road, Box 94, Chalfont 18914; phone (215) 249–9058.

Penn Shore Vineyards, 10225 East Lake Road, North East 16428; phone (814) 725–8688; fax (814) 725–8689.

Philadelphia Wine Company, 3061 Miller Street, Philadelphia 19134; phone (215) 482–3457.

Pinnacle Ridge Winery, 407 Old Route 22, Kutztown 19530; phone (610) 756–4481; fax (610) 756–4481; pinridge@aol.com.

Presque Isle Wine Cellars, 9440 Buffalo Road, North East 16428; phone (814) 725–1314; fax (814) 725–2092; prwc@erie.net; erienct/--prwc.

Quaker Ridge Winery, 211 South Wade Avenue, Washington 15301; phone (412) 222–2914; camconet.com/quakerridge.

Sand Castle Winery, River Road, Box 177, Erwinna 18920; phone (800) 722–9463; fax (610) 294–9174; winesand@aol.com.

Seven Valleys Vineyard, R.D. 4, Box 4660, Glen Rock 17327; phone (717) 235–6281; fax (717) 235–6281.

Slate Quarry Winery, 460 Gower Road, Nazareth 18064; phone (610) 759–0286; fax (610) 746–9684; sidswine@aol.com.

Smithbridge Cellars, 159 Beaver Valley Road, Chadds Ford 19317; phone (610) 558–4703; highgate@csrlink.net; smithbridge.com.

Susquehanna Valley Winery, 802 Mount Zion Drive, Danville 17821; phone (800) 326–9881; fax (717) 275–5813.

Twin Brook Winery, 5697 Strasburg Road, Gap 17527; phone (717) 442–4915.

Vynecrest Winery, 172 Arrowhead Lane, Breinigsville 18031; phone (800) 361–0725; fax (610) 398–7525.

West Hanover Winery, 7646 Jonestown Road, Harrisburg 17712; phone (717) 652–3711; fax (717) 651–0409; whwinery,@aol.com.

Windgate Vineyards Hemlock Acres, R.D. 1, Smicksburg 16256; phone (412) 963–9232; smicksburg-dayton.com.

Winery at Wilcox, Box 39, Mefferts Run Road, Wilcox 15870; phone (814) 929–5598; fax (814) 929–5598.

Appendix II

Tourism Promotion Agencies

Places to find additional information about Pennsylvania—where, they say, memories last a lifetime.

PENNSYLVANIA

Phone: (800) 847–4872

Web site: www.pavisnet.com

ADAMS COUNTY

Gettysburg Convention & Visitors Bureau

35 Carlisle Street

Gettysburg, PA 17325

Phone: (717) 334–6274

Fax: (717) 334–1166

ALLEGHENY COUNTY

Greater Pittsburgh Convention and Visitors Bureau

Four Gateway Center, Eighteenth Floor

Pittsburgh, PA 15222

Phone: (412) 281–7711 or (800) 366–0093 (Continental U.S. & Canada)

Fax: (412) 644–5512

E-mail: info@gpConvention and Visitors Bureau.org

ARMSTRONG COUNTY

Armstrong County Tourist Bureau

402 East Market Street

Kittanning, PA 16201

Phone: (724) 548–3226 or (888) 265–9954 (Continental U.S.)

Fax: (724) 545–7050

E-mail: armscopd@alltel.net

BEAVER COUNTY

Beaver County Tourist Promotion Agency

215B Ninth Street

Monaca, PA 15061

Phone: (724) 728–0212; (800) 564–5009 (in area code 724); or (800) 342–8192

Fax: (724) 728–0456

E-mail: tking@co.beaver.pa.us

Web site: www.co.beaver.pa.us

BEDFORD COUNTY

Bedford County Visitors Bureau

141 South Juliana Street

Bedford, PA 15522

Phone: (814) 623–1771or (800) 765–3331

Fax: (814) 623–1671

E-mail: bccvb@bedford.net

BERKS COUNTY

Reading and Berks County Visitors Bureau

352 Penn Street

Reading, PA 19602

Phone: (610) 375–4085 or (800) 443–6610

Fax: (610) 375–9606

BLAIR COUNTY

Allegheny Mountains Convention and Visitors Bureau

Logan Valley Mall

Route 220 and Goods Lane, Altoona, PA 16602

Phone: (814) 943–4183 or (800) 84–ALTOONA

Fax: (814) 943–8094

Web site: www.alleghenymountains.com

BRADFORD COUNTY

Endless Mountains Visitors Bureau

712 Route 6 East, Tunkhannock, PA 18657–9232

Phone: (570) 836–5431or (800) 769–8999 (U.S./Canada/Puerto Rico)

Fax: (570) 836–3927

Web site: www.endlessmountains.org

BUCKS COUNTY

Bucks County Conference and Visitors Bureau

152 Swamp Road

Doylestown, PA 18901

Phone: (215) 345–4552 or (800) 836–2825 (Continental U.S.)

Fax: (215) 345–4967

E-mail: buckscounty@bccvb.org

BUTLER COUNTY

Butler County Tourism Promotion Agency

201 South Main Street

Butler, PA 16003-1082

Phone: (724) 283–2222 or (888) 741–6772

Fax: (724) 283–0224

E-mail: chamber@isrv.com

Web site: www.butlercountychamber.com/tourism.htm

CAMBRIA COUNTY

Greater Johnstown/Cambria County Convention and Visitors Bureau

111 Market Street

Johnstown, PA 15901

Phone: (814) 536–7993 or (800) 237–8590 (Continental U.S./Canada)

Fax: (814) 539–3370

Web site: www.visitjohnstownpa.com

CAMERON COUNTY

Cameron County Tourist Promotion Agency

Croffwood Mills Building

P.O. Box 118

Driftwood, PA 15832

Phone: (814) 546–2665 or (888) 252–2872

CARBON COUNTY

Carbon County Tourist Promotion Agency

Railroad Station,

P.O. Box 90

Jim Thorpe, PA 18229

Phone: (570) 325–3673 or (888) 546–8467

Fax: (570) 325–5584; E-mail: carbon@jtasd.k12.pa.us

CENTRE COUNTY

Centre County Convention and Visitors Bureau

1402 South Atherton Street

State College, PA 16801

Phone: (814) 231–1400 or (800) 358–5466

Fax: (814) 231 8123

CHESTER COUNTY

Chester County Tourist Bureau

601 Westtown Road, Suite 170

West Chester, PA 19382-4536

Phone: (610) 344–6365 or (800) 228–9933

Fax: (610) 344–6999

CLARION COUNTY

Northwest Pennsylvania's Regional Visitors Bureau

175 Main Street

Brookville, PA 15825

Phone: (814) 849–5197 or (800) 348–9393

Fax: (814) 849–1969

CLEARFIELD COUNTY
See Clarion County

CLINTON COUNTY
Clinton County Economic Partnership

212 North Jay Street, Lock Haven, PA 17745

Phone: (570) 748–5782

Fax: (570) 893–4098

E-mail: tourism@cub.kcnet.org

COLUMBIA COUNTY
Columbia-Montour Tourist Promotion Agency

121 Paper Mill Road

Bloomsburg, PA 17815

Phone: (570) 784–8279 or (800) 847–4810

Fax: (570) 784–1166

CRAWFORD COUNTY
Crawford County Convention and Visitors Bureau

211 Chestnut Street

Meadville, PA 16335

Phone: (814) 333–1258 or (800) 332–2338

Fax: (814) 333–9032

DAUPHIN COUNTY

Harrisburg-Hershey-Carlisle Tourism and Convention Bureau

25 North Front Street

Harrisburg, PA 17101

Phone: (717) 231–7788 or (800) 995–0969

Fax: (717) 231–7790

E-mail: hhcConvention and Visitors Bureau@epix.net

DELAWARE COUNTY

Delaware County Convention and Visitors Bureau

200 East State Street, Suite 100

Media, PA 19063

Phone: (610) 565–3679 or (800) 343–3983

Fax: (610) 565–0833

ELK COUNTY

Elk County Visitors Bureau

119 Teaberry Road

P. O. Box 838

St. Marys, PA 15857

Phone: (814) 834–3723

Fax (814) 834–3725

E-mail: elkcovb@ncentral.com

ERIE COUNTY

Erie Tourist and Convention Bureau

1006 State Street

Erie, PA 16501

Phone: (814) 454–7191

Fax: (814) 459–0241

E-mail: erie-tourism@erie.net

FAYETTE COUNTY
See Somerset County

FOREST COUNTY

Forest County Tourism Promotion Agency

Box 608

Tionesta, PA 16353

Phone: (814) 755–3535 or (800) 610–6611

Web site: www.forestcounty.com

FRANKLIN COUNTY
See Lebanon County

FULTON COUNTY

Fulton County Tourist Promotion Agency

112 North Second Street

P.O. Box 141

McConnellsburg, PA 17233

Phone: (717) 485–4064

Fax: (717) 485–0322

E-mail: tpa@innernet.net

GREENE COUNTY

Greene County Tourist Promotion Agency

19 South Washington Street

Waynesburg, PA 15370

Phone: (724) 627–8687

Fax: (724) 627–8017

Web site: www.greenepa.net

HUNTINGDON COUNTY

Raystown County Visitors Bureau

RD 1, Box 222A

7 Points Road

Hesston, PA 16647

Phone: (814) 658–0060 or (888) 729–7869 (Continental U.S.)

Fax: (814) 658–0068

E-mail: ConventionandVisitorsBureau@raystown.org

INDIANA COUNTY

Indiana County Tourist Bureau

2090 Route 286 South

Indiana, PA 15701

Phone: (724) 463–7505

Fax: (724) 465–3819

E-mail: bshaf@microserve.net

JUNIATA COUNTY

Juniata-Mifflin Counties Tourist Promotion Agency

3 West Monument Square

Lewistown, PA 17044

Phone: (717) 248–6713

Fax: (717) 248–6714

Web site: www.juniatavalley.org

LACKAWANNA COUNTY

Pennsylvania's Northeast Territory Visitors Bureau

300 Penn Avenue, Scranton, PA 18503

Phone: (570) 963–6363 or (800) 229–3526 (Continental U.S.)

Fax: (570) 963–6852

LANCASTER COUNTY

Pennsylvania Dutch Convention and Visitors Bureau

501 Greenfield Road

Lancaster, PA 17601

Phone: (717) 299–8901 or (800) 723–8824

Fax: (717) 299–0470

E-mail: nspdConventionandVisitorsBureau@aol.com

LAWRENCE COUNTY

Lawrence County Tourist Promotion Agency

Cilli Central Station

229 South Jefferson Street

New Castle, PA 16101

Phone: (724) 654–8408 or (888) 284–7599

Fax: (724) 654–2044

E-mail: tourlc@ncconnect.com

LEBANON COUNTY

Pennsylvania's Rainbow Region Vacation Bureau

P.O. Box 329

625 Quentin Road

Lebanon, PA 17042

Phone: (717) 272–8555

Fax: (717) 272–8850

E-mail: michelle@parainbow.com

Web site: www.parainbow.com

LEHIGH COUNTY

Lehigh Valley Convention and Visitors Bureau

2200 Avenue A

Bethlehem, PA 18017

Phone: (610) 882–9200 or (800) 747–0561 (Continental U.S.)

Fax: (610) 882–0343

E-mail: mabungerz@lehighvalleypa.org

Web site: www.lehighvalleypa.org

LUZERNE COUNTY

Luzerne County Tourist Promotion Agency

56 Public Square

Wilkes-Barre, PA 18701

Phone: (570) 819–1877 or (888) 905–2872

Fax: (570) 819–1882

LYCOMING COUNTY

Lycoming County Visitors Bureau

454 Pine Street

Williamsport, PA 17701

Phone: (570) 326–1971 or (800) 358–9900 (Continental U.S.)

Fax: (570) 321–1208

E-mail: wlcc@naccess.net

Web site: www.williamsport.org/visitpa

MCKEAN COUNTY

Allegheny National Forest Vacation Bureau

Box 371

Bradford, PA 16701

Phone: (814) 368–9370

Fax: (814) 368–6778

E-mail: ldevlin01@aol.com

Web site: www.allegheny-vacation.com

MERCER COUNTY

Mercer County Convention and Visitors Bureau

835 Perry Highway

Mercer, PA 16137

Phone: (724) 748–5315 or (800) 637–2370

Fax: (724) 748–5533

E-mail: mcConventionandVisitorsBureau@pathway.net

Web site: www.merlink.org

MIFFLIN COUNTY
See Juniata County

MONROE COUNTY

Pocono Mountains Vacation Bureau

1004 Main Street

Stroudsburg, PA 18360

Phone: (570) 421–5791; (717) 424–6050; or (800) 762–6667

Fax: (570) 421–6927

MONTGOMERY COUNTY

Valley Forge Convention and Visitors Bureau

600 West Germantown Pike, Suite 130

Plymouth Meeting, PA 19462

Phone: (610) 834–1550 or (888) 847–4883

Fax: (610) 834–0202

MONTOUR COUNTY
See Columbia County

NORTHAMPTON COUNTY
See Lehigh County

NORTHUMBERLAND COUNTY
See Union County

PERRY COUNTY
See Dauphin County

PHILADELPHIA COUNTY

Philadelphia Convention and Visitors Bureau

1515 Market Street, Suite 2020

Philadelphia, PA 19102

Phone: (215) 636–1666 or (800) 537–7676

Fax: (215) 636–3327

PIKE COUNTY
See Monroe County

POTTER COUNTY

Potter County Visitors Association

P.O. Box 245

Coudersport, PA 16915-0245

Phone: (814) 435–2290; (814) 435–8230; or (888) POTTER2

Fax: (814) 435–8230

E-mail: potter_county@juno.com

Web site: www.pavisnet.com/pcva/

SCHUYLKILL COUNTY
Schuylkill County Visitors Bureau
91 South Progress Avenue
Pottsville, PA 17901
Phone: (570) 622–7700 or (800) 765–7282 (Continental U.S.)
Fax: (570) 622–8035

SNYDER COUNTY
See Union County

SOMERSET COUNTY
Laurel Highlands Visitors Bureau
120 East Main Street
Ligonier, PA 15658
Phone: (724) 238–5661 or (800) 925–7669
Fax: (724) 238–3673

SULLIVAN COUNTY
See Bradford County

SUSQUEHANNA COUNTY
See Bradford County

TIOGA COUNTY
Tioga County Visitors Bureau
114 Main Street, Suite 203
Wellsboro, PA 16901
Phone: (570) 724–0635 or (888) 846–4228
Fax: (570) 724–5084
Web site: www.visittiogapa.com

UNION COUNTY

Susquehanna Valley Visitors Bureau

R.R. 3-219D Hafer Road

Lewisburg, PA 17837-9714

Phone: (570) 524–7234 or (800) 525–7320

Fax: (570) 524–7282

VENANGO COUNTY

Oil Heritage Region Tourist Promotion Agency

P.O. Box 128

Oil City, PA 16301

Phone: (814) 677–3152 or (800) 483–6264 (Continental U.S)

Fax: (814) 677–5206

Web site: www.usachoice.net/oilregiontourist

WARREN COUNTY

Northern Alleghenies Vacation Region

315 Second Avenue

P.O. Box 804

Warren, PA 16365

Phone: (814) 726–1222 or (800) 624–7802

Fax: (814) 726–7266

E-mail: tna@penn.com

Web site: www.users.penn.com/~tna/

WASHINGTON COUNTY

Washington County Tourism Promotion Agency

1500 West Chestnut Street

Washington, PA 15301

Phone: (724) 228–5520 or (800) 531–4114

Fax: (724) 228–5514

Web site: www.washpatourism.org

WAYNE COUNTY
See Monroe County

WESTMORELAND COUNTY
See Somerset County

WYOMING COUNTY
See Bradford County

YORK COUNTY

York County Convention and Visitors Bureau

1 Market Way East

York, PA 17401

Phone: (717) 848–4000 or (800) 673–2429

Fax: (717) 843–6737

Web site: www.yorkpa.org

Index

INDEX

INDEX

INDEX

About the Author

Susan Perloff is a writer, writing coach, and writing-workshop leader. She runs writing workshops for corporations, advertising agencies, and non-profit organizations and runs writers' support groups for individuals.

Many years ago she served the City of Philadelphia as a municipal tour guide.

For four years Susan wrote a column on writing for the *Philadelphia Business Journal.* Her by-line has appeared in more than one hundred periodicals, including more than eighty times in the *Philadelphia Inquirer,* and she has won three national writing awards. She specializes in nonfiction. She has written promotional copy—annual reports, brochures, newsletters, flyers, etc. —for one hundred Philadelphia-area companies and organizations. This is her first book.